Victorious

On & Beyond the Mat

Trevor Lane

"There is always room in our broken world for great stories that inspire; stories that make us smile at adversity and help us to encourage others to do the same. That's the story of my friend, Trevor Lane. When I first encountered this remarkable young man, I realized I was meeting one of God's choicest servants. Trevor has hurdled many obstacles in his life and his astounding testimony will help you do the same. So, get ready to read a story that rises above the average; one that soars and inspires. It's what spending time with Trevor will do for your heart!" – Joni Eareckson Tada, *Joni and Friends International Disability Center*

I have had the honor of watching the verse, "I can do all things through Christ who strengthens me" lived out faithfully before me in the life of Trevor Lane! From his conversion to his call to ministry, this young man has trusted fully in the strength and wisdom of God. Little wonder that God is anointing and using his life and ministry in such a powerful and meaningful way. I am truly blessed to recommend his testimony to you in the form of Victorious: On and beyond the mat! – Tim Throckmorton, *Midwest Regional Director for Church Ministries for the Family Research Council*

"This book, and it's author, Trevor Lane will inspire and encourage every person who reads it. Trevor shows us that no matter what we face in this fallen world, God's grace is great enough to help us overcome. He also inspires us to attempt great things and never give up, no matter how many times we lose a match. Buy several copies of this book and give it to as many young people as possible." – Jeff Keaton, *President and CEO of Renewanation*

"Victorious is the name of the book, and Victorious is what you experience as you read it. Trevor Lane's testimony of God's power and Grace will bless you beyond measure! Please read this book and then share it with someone else. Anyone who reads this powerful story will be blessed and will be more Victorious." – Bob Burney, *Talk Show Host, 880am & 104.5fm The Word*

"If you've been tempted to give up in the face of challenges that come your way, this book is for you. Trevor's story of perseverance will inspire you to keep going. I can endorse this book not just because the contents are engaging and edifying (I especially love the "Beyond the Mat" sections), but also because I (as a mentor and professor) have seen Trevor successfully (with excellence) persevere in his ministry preparation at God's Bible School. His determination through his early life established a character of faithfulness that has helped him overcome the challenges of academic work and ministry development, while giving God the glory." -- Dr. Mark Bird, *Professor of Systematic and Practical Theology, God's Bible School and College*

Copyright © 2020 by Kindle Digital Publishing.

Without written permission of the publisher.

All Rights Reserved.

No part of this book may be used or reproduced by any means, graphic, electronic, or mechanical, including photocopying, recording, taping, or by any information storage retrieval system without the written permission of the publisher

Scripture references are taken from the New King James Version, King James Version, New American Standard Bible and New International Version. © 2020. All rights reserved.

Cover design by Jennifer Perkins

Dedication

This book is dedicated to my Lord and Savior Jesus Christ and to all the amazing people who spent countless numbers of hours shaping and molding me into the person I am today – both my physical well-being as well as spiritual.

In memory of Lesley Liston

1968 – 2016

Thanks for cheering all of us kids on.

The Empty Seat

Trevor Lane

There once was an old wooden chair

And ye who occupied it a kind thoughtful soul

Outspoken and bold what you thought she did not care

Surrounding this old wooden chair seating the beautiful soul, loved ones sharing a meal

Christmas, Easter and every holiday in between

We gather around an old wooden dining table

Sit on old wooden chairs and delve into grandma's home cooked meal

Voices running amuck usually filled with laughter

But now one voice is silenced

The wooden chair that once held the beautiful soul is now empty

For now who will occupy it, there is none but one

No one knows why God took you so soon

No one can fill the seat you occupied in the lives of those who loved you

But one day we will all gather together once again

And that old wooden chair will be occupied once more.

Table of Contents

Preface   10

Foreword   11

Prologue   12

Laying the Foundation   29

Rude Awakening   38

No Guts No Glory   55

The Streak   64

The Birth of the Crossface   72

There's a New Sheriff in Town   76

Déjà Vu   85

A Brave Chippewa   96

A Brave Chippewa Part II   102

Entering the Big Leagues   112

The Underdog Strikes   122

Setbacks   128

Winning Isn't Everything   134

Return to Central Michigan   139

Everything's an Illusion   149

Redeemed   152

Pushed to the Limit	*159*
The Power of Social Media	*170*
Casper the Ghost Returns	*173*
A Ride to Remember	*178*
Lights! Camera! Action!	*183*
The First of Many Last Times	*196*
Crossroads of Destiny	*200*
Angels Among Us	*206*
An Unstoppable Will	*208*
A Brave Send-off	*214*
Full Circle	*218*
LEaving A LEgacy	*223*
Epilogue	*228*
Final Thought	*238*
About the Author	*248*

Preface

This book, at its core, is a story of not only what a good support system of friends and family can do for a single person, but it's also a demonstration of the power of God through a life of struggle. I have asked several key people in my life to take part in this project with me and it is my hope that as you read my story, you will see the hand of God working in every circumstance.

James 1:2 – 4 says, "My brethren, count it all joy when you encounter various trials, knowing that the testing of your faith produces endurance. And let endurance have its perfect result, so that you may be perfect and complete, lacking in nothing" (NASB). Whatever you may be facing I hope this book gives you hope and reminds you that God is there for you too!

Foreword

Dan Coy

There are people we meet along the way in life that change us profoundly! I remember a young man that would come into our local church and would set near the back each week, proudly dressed in his high school jersey. I don't remember him saying much but he would come faithfully to worship each week.

God had another level in mind just around the bend for this young man! Trevor has impacted me from the moment God allowed our paths to cross! I am excited for you to read this story of God's life changing power in a fully surrendered young life. Trevor has experienced not only victory over cerebral palsy, but God has set him free to do what he was designed to do in life! You have the same God-given potential and God has another level for you, too!

Thank you, Trevor, for sharing your story with us and living out your God-given purpose. You inspire us all to find that level!

All in,

Dan Coy,

Sr. Pastor

Crossroads Church, Circleville, OH

Prologue

November 26th, 1997 – May 2010

For You formed my inward parts; You covered me in my mother's womb. I will praise You, for I am fearfully and wonderfully made; Marvelous are Your works…

Psalm 139:14 – 15 (NKJV)

I don't know where my passion for wrestling came from; I guess it was always there, I just had to look really hard. I had always been into professional wrestling, like The Undertaker, John Cena, people like that. I enjoyed watching it, but there was a part of me that wanted to be a part of something great, something that I wanted to be as important to me as family.

Before I tell you my story, I must first tell you the story behind the story. I was born with cerebral palsy, which is a condition where my brain and muscles tend to disagree. This causes the muscles in my legs to constantly be contracted. Because my muscles are always so tight, I have to stretch regularly just so I can move with minimal pain.

There are multiple underlying causes for developing CP, but mine was premature birth-- four months premature to be exact. My scheduled due date was supposed to be March 16, 1998, but instead I was born on November 26, 1997. This caused a lack of oxygen to my brain which caused the cerebral palsy.

There are many different types and levels of severity in CP, ranging from very mild, where you are able to get around and communicate well with others, to being bound to a wheelchair and requiring 24-hour care. CP can also affect speech and many other senses and organs throughout the body. My case, for example, would be considered mild. It affects the left side of my body more than my right side and I can communicate well with others. However, it has not always been this way.

As I mentioned previously, I was born four months premature which brought about many complications. I had many underdeveloped organs, which led to both of my lungs collapsing on three separate occasions. I also had a brain bleed and a staph infection in my blood. The doctors said I wouldn't survive, and even if I did survive, I would be a vegetable my entire life and never walk. Well, I did survive and after spending three months in the NICU, I was able to come home. Still, my parents were advised that I would never walk, and I would require around the clock care.

To the doctor's surprise, it didn't turn out like they had planned. By the time I was two years old, I was walking around on a walker and giving my parents a run for their money. The improvement didn't stop there. After a lot of excruciating physical therapy, I was able to retire the walker and graduate to forearm crutches! Forearm crutches are crutches that have a cuff at the base where your forearm slides through, (hence the name) and a handle in the middle to maintain balance.

While these contraptions may sound like the Holy Grail for people with physical disabilities, they aren't all they're cracked up to be. First of all, if you were to fall, which I did quite often, you would literally have to throw your crutches as you were falling or risk breaking your arms. Maneuvering stairs was next to impossible: it was like playing Russian roulette. To say I hated those things would be an understatement.

While I was enjoying a season of astounding progress, even though I hated the forearm crutches, I still had my fair share of roadblocks along the way. As a toddler starting preschool, I was very shy and timid and seemed isolated from the rest of the world. I had slurred speech and I had to be assisted with almost everything except eating. Consequently, this caused a delay in my life skills development that many people take for granted.

I can recall one time while lining up to go inside from recess, I was walking in single file with the rest of my class when the terrain went from flat to hilly. I wasn't able to sense the difference in time, and my crutch slid out from underneath me and I cracked my head on the blacktop, giving me a gash just above my left eyebrow that would require stitches. My mom picked me up and took me to the hospital. I don't remember the ride to the hospital, but I do remember laying on the hospital bed and the doctor putting the stitches in before the numbing medicine took effect. The pain was excruciating!

On top of that, because my muscles were so tight, I had to get regular Botox injections. Botox injections are needle injections used to relax muscles in the body, most commonly used in the face. In my case, doctors used Botox to try to relax the muscles in my legs. They would take a needle about six inches long and jam it into my leg. It didn't stop there. After they stuck the needle in, they would dig the needle around inside the muscle until they found the area they wanted. Only then they would inject the medicine.

I vividly remember the immense pain and my mother and other doctors having to restrain me as I cried and screamed until my throat was raw. That's why I cringe every time I hear of women wanting to get Botox for their face just to look a few years younger. I would gladly accept the fact that I'm getting older over Botox any day.

The Journey Begins

It was August of 2003, which meant I was finally ready to start my first day of kindergarten! I was still on crutches and had been for about a year and a half at this point, but I'm as rambunctious as any five-year-old. I was a bit nervous as you could probably imagine, leaving behind all the friends I had made and starting completely over. The one thing that calmed my nerves though was sitting on my grandma's lap.

While waiting for the bus, I noticed an old red song book sitting on the shelf. I opened it up to a random page and found the 'Star Spangled Banner.' I climbed onto my grandma's lap and asked if we could sing it. Thus, began our morning tradition of singing the Star-Spangled Banner and the Twelve Days of Christmas. Our masterful duet made me forget about the approaching school bus, which in my mind came much too quickly.

When I got on the bus, I didn't say anything. I just looked at the bus driver and she instructed me to sit in seat one so it will be easier for me to get off the bus. Suddenly, she got up from her seat and buckled me to a harness that was attached to my seat. Because of my cerebral palsy, it was difficult for me to sit upright so the harness was necessary to keep me sitting up straight. I noticed that everybody on the bus could see me and everybody was staring at me. That dagger-like stare I had come to know at such a tender age. Nobody else was confined to his seat, just me. In that moment, I realized just how different I was from everybody else.

The ride to the school was silent. Being the first day of kindergarten, not very many kids knew each other. The only sounds you could hear were the high-pitched whining of the brakes as the bus came to a stop and the pitter patter of little children's feet climbing the steps to get on the bus. You could even hear the stop sign lights on the bus as they flickered on and off.

The bus finally arrived at the school after what seemed like an eternity, but it was only about ten minutes. I was eager to get off the bus after being ensnared in the harness, but I had to wait until all of the other kids got off to avoid being trampled. The kids snuck glances of me as they walked past, like I was some sort of zoo animal. As I went to get off the bus, a woman stood in front of me, blocking my path. She was a rather large woman, her face featured numerous freckles and deep brown eyes. She wore a beaded necklace that seemed to go on forever down her torso and a beautiful multi-colored shirt and blue jeans.

"Hi," she said nervously. "I'm going to be your helper. You can call me Mrs. Jeanie or Mrs. Notestone, whatever you like."

I didn't say anything I just stared at her like she was some weird creature I had never seen before.

"Here, let me help with your crutches so you can get off the bus," she insisted. I handed her my crutches, but again I didn't say anything. I just didn't know what to think. We got inside and ventured down a long hallway. About halfway down the hall, we stopped, and she led me to the first door to the left. Before opening the door, Mrs. Jeanie turned to me and said, "You're going to love kindergarten."

As soon as she opened the door, out popped a middle-aged woman with dark curly hair, wearing eyeglasses. She wore a dark green sweater with a cross hanging around her neck, a pair of white trousers and she was surrounded by kids.

"Hi, I'm Mrs. Green," she said. "I'm going to be your teacher."

Mrs. Jeanie led me inside a room that was decorated with all sorts of colors, numbers, pictures of planets, the months of the year and a calendar. Almost as soon as I walked in the room. I felt the icy stare of curiosity piercing me once again. It's kind of hard not to notice a kid whose legs are crossed, who walks with two metal poles and has weird braces around his feet.

As I made my way over to the carpet to join the other kids, their eyes continued to follow me. I sat down on the floor as we awaited instruction. Suddenly, I felt a tiny finger prod the back of my shoulder. I looked behind me to find the source of the tactile interaction and saw a kid sporting dirty blonde hair and baby blue glasses.

"Hi, my name is Thomas," he said. "What's yours?"

I just continued to stare at the floor for what seemed like forever until I finally said in the softest voice possible, "T- Trevor."

"Oh, hey Trevor. Uh, what's wrong with your legs?" Thomas asked curiously. He seemed to study me for a long time, I assume waiting for an answer.

"I-I w-was born like this," I stuttered. I couldn't give him a better answer than, all I knew was that I was born with it and would have it for the rest of life.

Once I got past the first day jitters, kindergarten wasn't that bad. I began to make friends who didn't distance themselves from me and liked me for who I was and not because they felt sorry for me. I always had someone to play with at recess and whenever I would fall, the whole class practically would come to my aid. Of course, being as independent as I am, I would often decline the offer and get up by myself. Although, it felt good to know people in my own age group cared about me so much and didn't look down on me like some sort of other-worldly creature.

Thomas and I quickly became the best of friends. We began to do everything together from eating lunch to playing at recess. One day during lunch break, Thomas and I were having a very in-depth discussion about a topic that is near and dear to a five-year-old boy's heart - llamas.

"Hey, Lommy-," I piped up. Amidst all the laughter, I instantly realized my slip of the tongue. I called Thomas Lommy instead of Tommy. We began to howl in laughter as Thomas realized my mistake.

"Lommy? My name isn't Lommy," he said in between laughs. After our mishap, we told everyone what happened, including our teachers and principal. I was never going to live it down.

From the time I was very young, my parents have always pushed me to be as independent as possible. In turn, I was quite the stubborn boy. I was out at recess one afternoon and I wanted to slide down the slide. However, Mrs. Green gave me firm orders that I can only slide down the slide if I had someone with me to make sure I didn't fall. In my five-year-old mind, that translated to she didn't think I could do it on my own, rather than looking out for my safety.

In order to get to the slide, you had to climb a ladder and climb a series of steps. If you didn't have good balance, there was a very good chance that you would fall. I waited until Mrs. Green was looking away, talking to the other teachers, and I made my way over to the ladder. Once I got to the ladder, I looked back to make sure Mrs. Green was still busy before I made my move. I placed my foot on the first rung and began to make the climb. I knew one foot was weaker than the other, so I just avoided my weaker side. After carefully balancing myself on each rung, I made it up the ladder.

I then turned and climbed the steps to get to the slide. I looked over and Mrs. Green still had not noticed. I grabbed ahold of the bar hanging above the slide and took in the view. I had never seen the playground from this high up before! I basked in the glory for too long, though because my eyes made contact with Mrs. Green's. Her eyes grew wide.

"Trevor! No! she screamed.

I quickly slid down before she made her way over to where I was.

"I told you not to go down the slide unless someone was with you," she lectured.

My little stunt cost me my recess the next day, but after that incident, I don't think she ever had someone go with me on the slide again. I gave Mrs. Green many challenges throughout the year, but she never gave up on me. It was yet another example of the impact that love and patience can have on a person.

Spring 2004

The year seemed to fly by. Before I knew it, spring had sprung, and everybody seemed to have a case of spring fever. Well, everyone except me. As a person with special needs, going to the doctor for evaluations is just a regular part of life. They do a physical examination, a cognitive examination, and all the fun stuff. I'm being sarcastic, of course: it wasn't fun at all! The doctors told my parents that the Botox shots were not as effective because my spasticity was getting worse and that surgery was the best option to find relief. This made me really nervous.

The morning of the surgery, I felt very uneasy. Waking up at 5:00 in the morning and the thought of having your legs cut open was terrifying, to say the least. The surgery involved literally cutting the hamstrings and Achilles tendons in both legs to alleviate some of the spasticity caused by CP. Upon arriving at the hospital, I was stripped and made to don a surgical gown. This fear was quickly becoming a reality. The surgeon came in and introduced himself as Dr. King, and I was placed on a gurney. As I was being wheeled away, a level of fear that I had never experienced was beginning to settle in. I was being separated from my parents to have a guy that I barely knew operate on my legs.

Once inside the operating room, the staff began to plug me into numerous machines. I had cords coming out of me from every direction. The next thing I knew, a nurse was injecting a strange liquid into my arm.

"We're going to give you some medicine to make you fall asleep," she said softly. "You won't feel a thing."

I gave her a look of concern. "Make sure it tastes good," I said. Mere seconds later, I felt myself slipping into a deep sleep. The next thing I remember, I was screaming at the top of my lungs for my parents. The doctors quickly rushed me to my room; I opened my eyes and caught a glance of my aunt and uncle before falling back to sleep. When I awoke the second time, the pain was unbearable. I couldn't move, and I soon realized that I was going to need help with almost everything.

A little while later, the physical therapist came in, and to my despair, I was told that I had to get out of bed. I sat up and attempted to swing my legs over the side of the bed, but it was no use. As soon as I tried to lift my legs up, searing, sharp pain began to radiate down my legs. It was as if someone had set them on fire and stabbed them with knives. After many failed attempts, I was finally able to get to my feet and take a few small steps with the aid of my crutches. After a short break, I stood up again and began to walk the hallway with a wheelchair following close behind me. I walked as long as I could before I collapsed into the chair from exhaustion.

"That was pretty impressive," the PT said. "You aren't supposed to be able to walk that far yet. We were only supposed to get you out of bed and you walked down the hall!"

As night fell, I began to regret my stubbornness. The pain was off the charts and no amount of pain medication brought relief. Somewhere within the night, I drifted off into a light sleep. I awoke the next morning still in a considerable amount of pain, but it was not as severe as the night before. To my surprise, my doctor came in and informed me that I was getting discharged after only one night in the hospital! However, I still had a long road ahead of me with months of rehab.

While I was rehabbing at home, Mrs. Green came to visit me and dropped off the assignments that I needed to complete, since I was going to miss the rest of the school year. She told me that she was happy to see me, and everyone missed me at school. It felt good to know people cared about me so much. I had made some truly great friends.

The end of May had arrived, the last day of school as a matter of fact, and I was finally able to go back to class! My legs were still in casts, but I was now able to get around pretty well with the help of my crutches. As I entered the front of the school with my grandma, I was nervous as to what people would think of my legs being in purple casts. My nerves were soon eased by a kid in my class coming out of the bathroom and, upon seeing me, he grinned from ear to ear and blurted out, "Hey, Trevor," completely bypassing my casted legs. He didn't care that I had a disability, all he cared about was his friend was finally back after being gone for a very long time.

My first year of elementary school was complete and it was finally time to get these casts off. If you've ever broken a leg, you can imagine how relieved I was to finally get them off! However, the battle wasn't over-- it was time for the real rehab to begin. It was extremely difficult and painful, but by the end of it all, I was able to take my first steps without any assistance of any kind! I was overjoyed that I wouldn't have to put up with that walker or those forearm crutches ever again!

Seven Years Later

Before I knew it, seven years had passed, and I was in sixth grade. I was walking as close to normal as I can get, and I was not shy at all. I'd strengthened my upper body tenfold, and what was astonishing is, after I was born, the doctors said I would never walk! I sure proved them wrong!

At the end of my sixth-grade year, I was getting ready to graduate from elementary school and head off to junior high. I had come a long way from that shy, timid kid and I was using my stubbornness in productive ways rather than being defiant. I had become pretty popular with everyone else in my class as well. With my physical health improving by the day and having earned the love and respect of my peers, things seemed like they could not get any better.

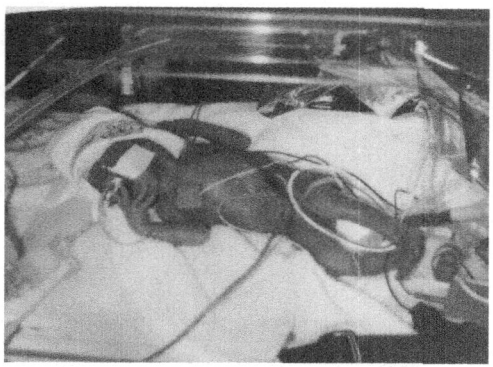

The day I was born – 11/26/1997

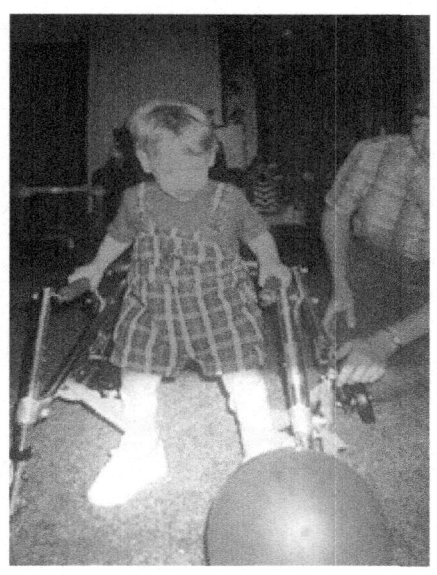

The day before my surgery. The note says, "Good luck, Trevor! We will miss you! We will see you next year!"

Cerebral palsy no restraint on Salt Creek Elementary School student

By MIKE PRATT
The Herald

One thing is relatively certain — Parents don't plan to need Department of Mental Retardation and Developmentally Disabled (MRDD) services for their children.

But Whisler's Rick and Lisa Lane say when their son Trevor was born four months premature with mild to moderate cerebral palsy they were thankful MRDD was available.

Trevor, now a first grader at Salt Creek Elementary School, has caught up to his peers in many respects and is able to make the grade in public school. His gait isn't as smooth as other boys his age, but it's probably going to be difficult for other children to rival his resolve.

He's had to work a little harder to do what other children do since he came into the world weighing a pound and a half.

Trevor's parents give much of the credit for preparing Trevor for public school to Brooks-Yates Center.

"Brooks-Yates came to us," his mother said. "We were happy about that because we wanted to do whatever we could to give Trevor as normal a life as we could. We wanted him to do what typical kids do, as much as he is able.

"We know he won't be able to play football or anything like that, but he will be able to run and play tag with his friends in school."

And Brooks-Yates Center

TREVOR LANE

helped prepare him for that.

"The people at Brooks-Yates asked if we would be interested in services," Lisa Lane said. "At that time, it was just physical therapy, doing the stretches. But that was something we wanted and needed, and we are grateful."

Trevor has been involved in early intervention services and preschool at Brooks-Yates from the time he was 6-months old.

"We just wanted what was best for Trevor," his mother said. "If it meant he would stay at Brooks-Yates, that was fine because we only wanted him to be as healthy and active as possible.

"If not for Brooks-Yates Center, Trevor would not be in public school.

There is no way we could have done for ourselves what this school has done for him."

Trevor still needs physical and occupational therapy, but this is the first year he hasn't

PICTURED ARE LISA and Rick Lane, with sons, Travis and Trevor.

had to continue speech therapy.

"He has caught up to his peers in speech," Lisa Lane said. "We have just been amazed with his progress almost every day.

"I really hadn't known anyone with cerebral palsy, but from what I had seen I thought a child would just exist. I had no idea there were different levels and he would have a chance to interact with typical children. Brooks-Yates helped us through that."

Having a premature baby

See LANES, Page 3

Lanes...

Continued from Page 1

never crossed Lane's mind when she became pregnant.

"I never would have dreamed we would have needed MRDD services," she said.

"You never think it will be your child, but that's the way it is. You never know when you're going to need MRDD services."

So what's the key to rearing a child with disabilities?

"Don't ever give up on your child," Lane said. "As long as you can get them the help they need there is hope."

7ᵗʰ Grade 2010-2011

1

Laying the Foundation

June 2010 – August 2010

Behold, I will do a new thing, now it shall spring forth; Shall you not know it? I will even make a road in the wilderness and rivers in the desert.

Isaiah 43:19 (NKJV)

"Trevor!" Mom yelled from the kitchen.

"Coming, Mom," I said. I quickly put on my shoes and raced to the back door.

"What took you so long?" Mom complained. "You know we're already late and I want to stop at the library."

As I mentioned before, I have cerebral palsy. This means my muscles do not respond right at times to some commands. To help strengthen my muscles, I went to physical therapy for the summer. My mom and I were on our way to therapy and I asked the question I have wanted to ask for a long time. I was transitioning from elementary to the junior high and I thought this would be the perfect time to ask.

"Mom, can I wrestle this year?"

"No," she yelled.

"But I think I could be really good at it," I fought back.

"You can't wrestle in your condition!" She's already told me this a hundred times, but for some reason, I thought this time would be different.

Once we pulled into the parking lot, we went in and Jada, my physical therapist took me back to the gym. As we worked, I told her what I was looking forward to the most as I transferred from the elementary to junior high. I took this opportunity to tell her I wanted to wrestle.

"You want to wrestle?" Jada asked, surprised.

"Yeah, but my mom won't let me," I said.

"Well, I guess we will have to change her mind, won't we?" Jada said, in that confident tone I had come to know over the years. It's almost as if Mom had supersonic hearing, because right as Jada said that, she walked in.

"What's going on?" she asked.

"Trevor here says he wants to wrestle. I think it would be really good for him," Jada said.

"But they're out for blood," mom argued. "Plus, I don't think he'll be able to keep up."

"Don't worry. At least let him try it, and if Trevor decides he doesn't like it, then he can stop, Jada said. "Plus, I think wrestling will help strengthen his legs a lot."

Mom thought for a moment, then sighed. "I suppose it's worth a shot."

"Yes!" I exclaimed. I was finally going to get to wrestle! It wasn't like what the guys on TV did, but it was close enough. I walked out of the therapy clinic happier than I had ever been. The next day I called my cousin, BJ (who is also a wrestler), to tell him the great news. It rang a few times before I heard his voice on the other end.

"Hello?" BJ answered.

"Guess what?" I asked excitedly.

"What?" BJ asked in suspense.

"Mom is letting me wrestle!" I said.

"No way!" he exclaimed.

"Yeah, way," I fired back. "I still have to check with the coach to make sure it's okay, but Mom said it was okay!"

"That's awesome!" BJ exclaimed.

A couple of days later, it was time for the junior high Open House and, while I was excited, I was also very nervous. It wasn't because I was going to a new school in the district, it was mostly because I was worried about whether the wrestling coach and team would like me or not. My mom and I walked into the building, and I wasn't concerned about getting my schedule, I wasn't worried about meeting my teachers; the only thing I was worried about was finding the wrestling coach. I knew the coach's name; his name was Mr. Hurd. I didn't know what he looked like, so Mom had to point him out to me. Coach Hurd was wearing a pair of tan khakis, a button-up dress shirt, glasses, and he wore a serious, intimidating look on his face.

"Hey, are you the wrestling coach?" I asked.

"Yes, I am," he said.

Then my mom stepped in, "He has cerebral palsy. Do you think he'll be to able wrestle?"

"Well, sure," said Coach Hurd. "What they do is they start out standing up, and then as the match progresses, they are on the mat," he continued. "So, of course, he'll be able to wrestle."

"Thank you so much!" I exclaimed.

As soon as I got the news, I went and told everyone I could. They were all very happy for me, but there was one person in particular I couldn't wait to tell. That was my best friend since kindergarten– Thomas Creech. I spotted Thomas off in the distance by the gym entrance. He was dressed casually he wore jeans and a t-shirt and an MMA hat.

"Hey, Creecher!" I yelled. We gave Thomas the nickname Creecher because he's big and muscular. He has legs as big as tree trunks, and as Hulk Hogan would say, "24-inch pythons brother!"

"Hey, what's up, Trev?" Thomas asked.

"Dude, guess what? I get to wrestle this year!"

"What? No way! That's awesome!" he said astonished. "I'm wrestling this year, too!"

"Sweet!" I said.

Middle school is going to be awesome!

Upon getting home that night, I couldn't wait to tell my Dad.

"Dad, I get to wrestle this year," I bellowed.

"Hmm," he grunted. "You are?"

My father is a heavier set man, a little on the short side and he is a pretty difficult person to read. He often wore the same expression on his face. It was really difficult to tell at times if he was happy, angry, or sad because he always wore the same expression on his face, no matter what mood he was in.

That night, I found it hard to go to sleep. It could have been the result of restless leg syndrome and insomnia due to CP or the fact that I was so excited about being able to wrestle. Either way, sleep was not in the cards. What little bit of sleep I managed to get, however, did not seem to affect my excitement level in the slightest. I wolfed down my breakfast and bolted out the door to anxiously await the arrival of the school bus. It wasn't until the bus arrived that the nerves started to arise.

What if the other kids don't like me?

What if they make fun of me?

What if I get kicked off the wrestling team because they don't think I'm good enough?

All these thoughts and more were running through my head. As we approached the school, the kid sitting beside me must have sensed my nervousness because he leaned in and asked me if this was my first day, to which I feverishly replied, "Yes."

"You'll be okay," he said.

His words brought me a little bit of comfort, but I was still feeling uneasy. I walked into the building and was practically swept away by a raging current of students trying to find their way to class. When I was finally able to break away from the chaos, my eyes beheld a maze of classrooms. I'd always heard stories about how kids would get lost the first few days of transitioning to the new school. At that moment, I understood why. After a few minutes of wandering like a lost puppy, I was eventually able to find my homeroom.

Upon taking my seat, the teacher got up from his desk and introduced himself. As he was talking, the intercom chimed, and the voice of the principal, Mrs. Lane, rang over the speakers. In case you were wondering, yes, she is related to me. She is my aunt. While that sounds awesome, it amplified the pressure of staying out of trouble. Not that I am the type that would cause trouble, but could you imagine that phone call home?

"Good morning, students," she began, "Welcome to the first day of school."

I zoned out as she began going through all of the introductory material, but then she said something that caught my attention.

"Open mats for wrestling will begin in September and will continue through the first day of practice." She added, "If you have any questions, please contact Coach Hurd."

"Ha! Wrestling is so stupid," someone piped up, "I don't understand how anyone would want to roll around with a bunch of sweaty guys."

I came to find out throughout the day that this was the stance that a lot of people took when it came to wrestling. But I didn't let that bother me. I had never competed in sports before, other than in Special Olympics and was too excited about the new chapter in my life that was about to begin to worry about what others thought. After all, how bad could it be?

Beyond the Mat

Jan Hurd

I first became aware of Trevor when he was a seventh-grade student at McDowell Exchange School. He seemed like a happy young man even with the hurdles he faced on a daily basis. I happened to be in the school office one day when the principal and a parent I did not know were talking. Trevor's mother was inquiring about ways to get him involved in non-academic activities. I had coached many sports and was the head wrestling coach for the high school at the time.

The principal, Mrs. Lane (Trevor's aunt), called me in and asked if I had any suggestions on sports for him. My first thought went to wrestling. I have witnessed many athletes with physical conditions that make most sports difficult excel in wrestling. As a matter of fact, when I was in my first year as the junior varsity coach, I had a young man that had CP.

Trevor got interested in the sport and worked as hard as anyone and refused to make excuses and did what every other wrestler did in practice. His work ethic and determination were inspirational for the other team members. After retirement, I didn't get to see much wrestling, but I noticed when there, that any time Trevor went on to the mat, almost every set of eyes were on him. He never disappointed and always gave his maximum effort.

Probably the most telling event that showed what an influence Trevor had on his fellow students and opponents was the night of his last home match and there were people there with signs for him. I have never seen anything like it in twenty-five years as a wrestling coach.

When he finished people were lining up to congratulate him and get their picture taken with him (me included). He taught an old coach an important lesson about the sport; wins are nice, but effort, integrity and determination make a person stand out among his peers.

Jan Hurd,
Logan Elm High School wrestling coach,
1986 – 2011

2

Rude Awakening

September 2010

"Your beginnings will seem humble, so prosperous will your future be."
Job 8:7 (NIV)

The final bell of the day rang, and I jumped from my seat and raced out the door. It was the first day of open mats and nothing was going to stop me. It was quite a trek from the middle school to the athletic complex, but my excitement soon outweighed my fatigue when I realized I was at the doorway. Upon walking inside the building, I was bombarded with the smell of what I can only describe as a mixture of sweat and rust.

The interior of the building was very much box-shaped, and the floor was covered with wrestling mats that stretched from one end of the building to the other. The walls had mats on them and the wall on the far end had a tree painted on it with LOGAN ELM going through it. However, what really caught my attention was the contents of the wall directly in front of me. It was bathed with pictures of what I assumed were past wrestlers.

Directly in the middle of the line of pictures was an Ohio-shaped plaque that read:

STATE PLACER

SHANE GIFFORD

2007 7th place 140lb.

2009 2nd place 152lb.

He must be really good if he placed at State, I thought.

I made my way to the locker room to change and, to my surprise and horror, there was somebody else in the locker room, changing. You may be thinking, "Why is that a big deal?" Well, normally it wouldn't be, but he was standing on a scale, completely naked, I might add.

"Hello," he said, as if nothing was out of the ordinary.

It suddenly felt like the first day of kindergarten all over again. Except this time, it was a little more awkward for obvious reasons.

"Hi," I said reluctantly.

"Is this your first time at open mats?" he asked.

"Uh-huh," I said.

"It's fun," he said. "You'll really enjoy it."

I sure hope so. Because, as of right now, I'm not liking what I'm seeing.

I got dressed and went to join the others who had already arrived. I began to stretch as the rest of the wrestlers began to introduce themselves to me. Everyone seemed friendly-- that was a relief. A couple of guys even tried to wrestle with me. I played along, even though I had no idea what I was doing.

As we were stretching, Coach Hurd walked in and informed everybody that we were running outside.

Coach Hurd pointed over to an old stationary bike and said, "Trevor, you can ride that bike over there if you want."

I obliged, because I knew I was probably not going to be able to keep up with the others. While the others made their way outside, I made my way over to the bike. I was able to get on it with no problem, but peddling was another story. Because of my cerebral palsy, my left foot always wants to stay flexed. As a result, my foot kept slipping off of the pedal when I tried to get it moving. I worked on just keeping my foot on the pedal for the entire half hour everybody was gone. Needless to say, I didn't get much of a warm-up in.

The others began to make their way back in, their bodies shining with sweat. Coach Hurd called us into a circle on the mat and he began to introduce himself and the others who were standing in the middle with him.

"Hi, everybody," Coach Hurd began. "My name is Coach Hurd and I am the head coach of the high school wrestling program. These two men standing beside me are Coach Barnes, he is the assistant wrestling coach at the high school, and Shane Gifford, who just graduated from Logan Elm and placed 2nd at State last year."

Coach Barnes is bald, with a heavier-set build, while Shane was average height and looked to have the body of a Greek god. Either way, I wouldn't want to mess with either one of them.

"Okay," Coach Hurd said, "today were going to start with the basics. We're going to do a drill called shuffle and shoot. To shuffle, all you have to do is get in a good stance, keep your butt low, and side step to the left or right when we tell you to. When taking a shot, you're going to keep your dominant leg forward and swing through with your other leg."

Shuffling was the easy part, I could do that, no problem. Taking the shot, however, that was a different story. I could step with my strong leg, but when I tried to swing through with my bad leg, it's like my body froze up on me and I would lose my balance and fall. I tried and tried again with no success. Feeling discouraged, I went and joined the circle to await Coach Hurd's next instructions.

"Everybody's shots are looking pretty good," Coach Hurd said. "Now, let's work on executing a takedown. The first thing you want to do is get in your stance. Then you want to circle with the guy. As soon as he opens up that far leg, we're going to shoot in with a high crotch. Once we've got the high crotch, we're going to drop down to the leg and drive in with our shoulder and follow him down to the mat."

I was a little nervous trying this for the first time. I didn't want to hurt anyone or me for that matter. My partner's name was Troy and it was his first year as well, so he was just as lost as I was. I didn't know whether to be relieved or terrified. Troy went first, and he shot in and grabbed my leg. I was unable to balance on one foot and Troy didn't even get my leg half way up before I fell and crashed to the mat with a thud.

"Sorry," I said. "I have trouble keeping my balance."

"It's okay," Troy assured. "Come on, it's your turn."

I was nervous trying out a takedown for the first time. How was I going to execute the move if I couldn't shoot? Just then, Coach Barnes came beside me.

"I know you can't use your legs very well," Coach Barnes said. "But you look like you're pretty strong in your upper body. Try getting as low as you can and then shooting in for the leg."

I did as he suggested. I squatted as low as I could and I grabbed Troy's leg. Now for the challenging part, I slowly stood up while holding Troy's leg and I quickly drove into him with my shoulder. The end result was Troy and me both crashing to the mat. Except Troy took the brunt of the impact. It worked! Before I had the opportunity to celebrate, Coach Hurd called us over to the far edge of the mat.

"We're going to do some conditioning, and Shane here is going to lead it," Coach Hurd said.

"Okay, I need everybody to form a line," Shane instructed. "We're going to have teams of two carry this punching bag from one end of the mat to the other. The next two people will go after the last two. Ready? Go!"

The first two guys blasted off like a rocket with the punching bag on their shoulders. They were down and back in what seemed like a split second and, while the second group seemed to have struggled a bit, being slow and wobbly, they made it.

"Let's go, push it!" Shane yelled.

What was Shane going to think of me? I can't run fast without resistance let alone a 150lb. punching bag on my shoulder and someone else running faster than I can.

There was an odd number of people, so Shane helped out the next guy in line. Shane took off but my attention wasn't on Shane. There was some weird substance on the mat. It was blood! Neither I nor anybody else was bleeding, from what I could see, so where could it be coming from? Shane and his partner had completed their run and returned to the locker room. A few seconds went by and all of a sudden, I heard a blood curdling scream. Shane hobbled out onto the mat and to my horror, I saw Shane's big toe hanging by a thread of skin and a trail of blood following close behind him.

"Call the squad!" Coach Barnes yelled.

The rest of us huddled together like a pack of scared puppy dogs while Shane was being helped over to the bench. A few minutes passed by and the situation has seemed to have calmed down. Then something unimaginable happens. Shane starts laughing! I couldn't believe it-- this poor man must be going into shock. No, that can't be it, because if he was going into shock, he wouldn't have his phone out taking pictures of his toe!

The squad arrived with the stretcher, which Shane refused and instead hobbled out to the squad himself.

That man is either the toughest guy in the world or the craziest.

Just then, my mom walks in with a panicked look on her face.

"Oh, thank God," she said, relieved. "I thought that squad was for you."

"So, how was your first open mat?" she asked.

I looked at her, I looked down at my feet and looked back at her.

"It is certainly one first that I will never forget."

First Day of Practice - *November 2010*

Despite the traumatic incident that occurred on my first day wrestling, I continued to go to open wrestling mats throughout the month of October. Some may think I am completely nuts, but besides that little mishap, I've thoroughly enjoyed wrestling whether I was getting my butt kicked or not. However, what surprised me the most was the fact that my mother continued to let me wrestle after the accident even though she did say those people wrestling were out for blood and were ripping their toes off. Mom always has been really protective of me, some could say a little too protective at times. She could have used this as the perfect excuse to not let me wrestle but for some reason she didn't.

October came and went, and before I knew it, November was here at last. Which meant it was time for wrestling season to officially begin! Even though, during the preseason, I got to know a lot of the people who were going to be wrestling, I was still a little nervous, because everyone who played football but also wrestled was going to be there, too. I couldn't help but wonder how they were going to treat me.

I walked inside of the wrestling barn and I was met by a younger man. He had a rather big build and a baby face complexion with Jesus-like hair.

"Hi, my name is Coach Landau," he said. He pointed over to where a big group of kids were sitting, "You can have a seat in the circle, then we'll get started."

"What's your name?" Coach Landau asked.

"Trevor." I said.

"Nice to meet you, Trevor," he said.

I went over to the circle and joined the others. While we were waiting, some of my teammates introduced themselves to me. They were friendly, and they didn't even ask me why I walked funny.

"Okay, guys, we're going to go ahead and get started," Coach Landau said. "What we're going to do is go around in a circle and introduce ourselves."

"My name is D.J White," one kid piped up. "I'm in 8th grade."

"My name is Dominic Vagnier," called out another. "I'm in 8th grade."

"My name is Micah Linton. I'm in 7th grade."

"My name is Dustin Miller. I'm in 7th grade."

"My name is Thomas Creech. I'm in 7th grade."

One by one, we all went around the circle until it eventually reached me.

"My name is Trevor Lane," I said. "I'm in 7th grade."

"Great job guys," Coach Landau said. "Let's get a warm-up run going."

A run? It's a chore for me to walk, let alone run, I thought.

I took off running along with the others and, to my horror, I glanced over and saw Coach Landau put ten minutes on the time clock. How was I ever going to survive? It wasn't long after that thought crossed my mind that I began to feel a burning sensation in my lungs. I looked over at the clock and realized only three minutes had passed. I was already slowing down and winded and there were still seven minutes left on the clock.

I am not going to sit here and pretend that I was the most in-shape guy in the room, because I wasn't. My cardio did need some work. However, people with cerebral palsy expend three to five times more energy than the average person to complete everyday tasks. This makes running extremely difficult, because my body is trying to use energy reserves it doesn't have. What made it even more difficult was the fact that I didn't have shoes on. I slid around as if I were on ice.

Finally, the clock hit zero and I was able to get a break.

"Okay, we're going to do warm-up drills," D.J. called out. "I need everyone to get in lines of four or five."

We all did as he instructed and D.J. called out the first drill, which was shots. We were supposed to take shots from one end of the mat to the other but every time I tried to take a shot and swing through with my left leg, I fell on my face. I tried and tried and tried again, each time producing the same result. Finally, Coach Landau told me that if there was anything that I couldn't do, to just run to the other end.

"Duck walks," D.J. called out.

What the heck is a duck walk? Were we going to waddle like a duck?

Unfortunately, it wasn't going to be that easy. A duck walk is a warm-up exercise in which you take multiple shots in rapid succession. I tried it, but unfortunately, it was déjà vu from the last exercise. If I was having this much difficulty with just the warm-up, how was I going to fare when the real practice began? I was able to do some of the exercises, such as the forward roll. However, I had to do it a little differently than the others. I was unable to tuck my head and roll, so as an alternative, I used my arms to propel myself forward. You either find an excuse or find a way.

Coach Landau called us into a circle to begin practice. Since this was our first day, he went over the basics that we covered during open mats. I couldn't wait to show my coaches what I could do. The group broke away and I scurried to find a partner. Coincidentally, I ended up with Troy again. We began to drill, and I attempted to perform a takedown the way Coach Barnes showed me. I completed all of the steps that equated to a nearly flawless takedown. Well, flawless for me, anyway.

"Great job Trev!" Coach McComas called out.

After a few minutes of drilling, Coach Landau called us back into the circle.

"Now that we've covered the basic takedown," Coach Landau began, "we're going to work from what's called the "Referees position." The opponent starts on his hands and knees and we wait for the referee's signal to mount," he paused for a moment before continuing. "Once we get the refs OK, we mount. The way you mount is you are angled a little bit so you're not directly behind the guy. You then wrap either your left or right arm around his belly, depending on which side you like better. Finally, you cup your left or right hand around his elbow."

Coach Landau called over one of the other coaches and continued his explanation. "What we're going to work on now is called a stand-up. This is a good bottom defense move if you're down and you need to get a quick point," he added. "So, I mount and Coach McComas is going to stand up."

"To stand up, you need to bring the leg forward on the side that your opponent doesn't have ahold of," Coach McComas chimed in. "When you stand up, you need to do it explosively in order to push back into your opponent. Once you're up, the guy is going to have your arm in what's called a 2-on-1. To break this, you're going to put both thumbs in between your arm and the guy's hands. Once you've broken the grip, turn in and face him."

The group broke away and Troy and I reunited. Troy got into position and I mounted on top. Troy quickly brought his leg up and pushed into me to help him stand up. If you haven't figured it out already, I'm not the best person to lean on for stability. I offer about as much stability as a three-legged table. I tried to stand up with him, but my body wouldn't allow me to react quickly enough. Thus, we both landed flat on our faces. Because I kept losing my balance, Troy had to practice with a different partner in order to do the move correctly. I knew I couldn't help it that I kept losing my balance, but it still frustrated me that I couldn't do the simplest of moves right.

Then, it was my turn to try. I got into position and I tried to bring my leg up but once I would get my leg up, I would fall over. As you might imagine, it was quite frustrating. Not only was this supposed to be a fairly simple move, but I was using my strong side to boot! Yet each time I would stand up, I would fall down. My frustration must have been visibly etched on my face because D.J hurried over to assist me.

"Try pushing up with your arms and then standing up." D.J suggested.

I did as he said and, with Troy on top of me, I pushed and exploded up just as someone who would be doing a normal stand up. Before I knew it, I was on my feet, but it wasn't time to celebrate just yet. I still hadn't done what was crucial to completing the sequence. Troy had my arm in a 2-on-1 and I had yet to break it. I slipped my two thumbs into the crease of his arm and I successfully broke the grip and turned into him. Despite all of the frustration, with the help of my teammate I was able to perform a move in my own special way. You either find an excuse or find a way.

"All right, time for some conditioning," Coach Landau yelled out. "I need everybody to form a line along the mat and we're going to sprint from one end of the mat to the other," he explained. "Ready? Go!"

We all blasted off in unison and took off for the wall. As I was running, I was tripped up by a gap in between the mats and a searing pain enveloped my big toe. Images of that fateful day when Shane ripped his toe off as a result of a similar circumstance flooded my mind. I hobbled over to Coach McComas in what I would describe as a calm panic.

"I think I tore my toenail off," I said.

Coach McComas looked surprised and said, "Let's see what the damage is."

With the greatest of care, I slowly removed my sock expecting the worst. Sure enough, I did sever my toenail, but the toe was still fully intact.

"At least it didn't end up like Gifford's," I laughed.

"Yeah, that's true," Coach McComas laughed back.

"All right, Coach Landau yelled. "We're going to play a game called trashcan basketball. The way we play this is we score just like we would in regular basketball, except you're on your knees and you can wrestle to try and steal the ball."

D.J and Dustin picked teams and we were ready to begin. I got down on my knees and Coach Landau threw the ball in the center. A dozen of us leaped onto the ball like a pack of wild dogs. I had my hands on the ball for a quick second, but before I knew it, I was blindsided by Thomas. He steamrolled me into the mat which ultimately caused me to let go of the ball. It was chaos and pandemonium! You would have thought it was the equivalent of the last morsel of food on earth and it was either eat or be eaten. The opposing team was willing to do whatever it took to score, it seemed, even if it cost us our lives.

Coach Landau must have been eager for somebody to score, because he joined in on the action. Of course, he had to be on the opposing team that I wasn't on. I was lost in thought, but I was quickly brought back to reality when I saw Coach Landau heading right for me. Thankfully, it wasn't me he was after, it was the ball.

"Hulk smash," Coach Landau cried out.

Before I knew it, a number of my teammates and I were flattened onto the mat like a common house fly under the sheer power of this man. As a result, D.J's team was able to make the winning basket. With that, we ended our first day of practice.

I very slowly and gingerly made my way to the locker room. I don't think I have ever pushed my body this hard and I was beginning to feel the effects. I stepped on the scale and it read *102 lbs* which meant I was going to be in the 104-pound weight class. I didn't think much of it at the time, so I put on my clothes and left. I walked outside, and my mom was already waiting for me. It took all of the strength I had left to be able to get in the car.

"How was your first day of practice," she asked.

"I got tackled by Coach Landau," I muttered.

Mom laughed as we drove away into the evening horizon.

Debut Match- *December 11, 2010*

Remember when I said I was in the 104-pound weight class? It turned out, that if you had someone who is in the same weight class as you on the team, you had to wrestle that person for the varsity spot. As luck would have it, I did have somebody else in my weight class; Micah Linton. It just so happens that he comes from a family of extremely talented wrestlers and, as you could guess, he beat me every time we wrestled.

Fortunately, Coach Landau said that they sometimes allow extra wrestlers to compete in tournaments and, when I found out that I was going to be able to wrestle in the next tournament, I could hardly contain my excitement! Sleep was difficult to achieve, my mind racing with possible scenarios that could take place. Was I going to be rookie of the year or fade away into obscurity before I even got started? Eventually, I was able to drift off to sleep.

I was awakened by the high-pitched whine of my alarm clock. Still in a groggy state, I glanced at the clock on my night-stand which read, 5:30 A.M.

What sane 13-year-old willingly gets up at 5:30 in the morning? I thought.

Nevertheless, my excitement was still boiling over. I got dressed, gathered my things and out the door I went. When I arrived at the wrestling barn. I was surprised to meet a sea of sleeping wrestlers sprawled out onto the mat.

"Go check your weight," D.J mumbled.

I was relieved when I stepped on the scale and it read 101 lbs. In wrestling, if you are even one tenth of a pound overweight, you won't be eligible to wrestle in the tournament. I walked out and saw a couple of my teammates running, trying to shed those last few ounces. It was then that I made a vow to myself that I would never be overweight the day of a tournament.

The bus arrived, and we all loaded up and set off for Amanda-Clearcreek Middle School. The bus ride there was quiet, as everyone was trying to catch up on lost sleep. When we arrived, we were rushed back to the locker room to begin weigh-ins. I was immediately told to strip down and directed to a line. After waiting for what seemed like an eternity, it was finally my turn. I stepped on the scale and it read 101 lbs, just as it did before. I made my weight class; now it was time to wait for the tournament to begin.

As the time drew near, my nerves got closer and closer to reaching a boiling point. The butterflies in my stomach would not relent and, before I knew it, it was time to warm up. As I was running, I glanced around the gymnasium and saw that people were beginning to file in. I noticed my parents sitting in the first section of bleachers, looking on intently.

A loud speaker blasted into the gymnasium. "Wrestlers, please clear the mats."

After the national anthem played, Coach Landau came up to me and informed me that I was going to be in one of the first matches. As we were making our way to the mat I was designated to wrestle on, my legs became shaky and felt like jelly.

"Are you nervous?" Coach Landau asked.

"Yeah," I said sheepishly.

Before I knew it, it was time for my match. I went over the table and they gave me a red band to put around my ankle. As I looked up, I saw my opponent standing before me. He looked like he meant business. Still shaky, I stepped to the center of the mat and shook his hand.

"Ready, wrestle," said the referee as he blew the whistle.

There was no time to react. My opponent tackled me to the ground and had my arms and legs snared so I couldn't fight back. I lay flat on my back, helpless. I wiggled and squirmed but to no avail, he had me trapped.

"1.. 2.. 3.. 4.. 5.." The ref began to count. A split second later, I heard the resounding smack as his hand collided with the mat. I had lost, it was over that quick. As I lay there trying to process what just happened, I found myself glaring at the lights.

"What the heck have I gotten myself into? I thought.

3

No Guts No Glory

December 2010

And not only that, but we also glory in tribulations, knowing that tribulation produces perseverance; and perseverance, character; and character, hope.

Romans 5:3 – 4 (NKJV)

I came across a unique quote by Dan Gable some time ago and I thought it fit the perception of wrestling perfectly. It goes like this:

"The first period is won by the best technician. The second period is won by the kid in the best shape. The third period is won by the kid with the biggest heart."

My other matches at the Amanda tournament were identical to my first. All three of my matches that day ended with the same result- me getting pinned and staring up at the lights. I could barely last the whole first period, let alone all three.

Our next wrestling match was against Circleville, our school's rival. I was determined to hone my craft, working harder than I ever had before. My teammates and coaches were outstanding in being patient with me and helping me adapt my own style of wrestling. Because of my cerebral palsy, my move set was limited. But I focused on what I could do well, instead of dwelling on what I couldn't do. I was able to execute a double leg takedown with such ferocity, it took whoever was on the receiving end by surprise. In the referee's position, I had mastered how to explode on bottom and get the escape. My confidence had increased ten-fold, it seemed, from the week prior.

Before I knew it, the day of the meet was upon us. To say I was eager to step onto the mat again would be an understatement. Unfortunately, I once again lost my wrestle-off against Micah, so that put me back in the junior varsity slot. Fortunately, just like the last tournament, this tournament also allowed extra wrestlers to compete. I couldn't wait to put my sharpened skills to the test.

When we arrived at the school, we went about the normal routine for a wrestling meet. We weighed in, we had our normal thirty-minute post-weigh-in pig-out session, and we warmed up. During warm-ups, I practiced all of the moves I had worked on that whole week.

I'm sure I'll be able to last all three rounds this time around. Maybe even win a match!

The loud-speakers came to life. "Wrestlers, please clear the mats."

The wonderful thing about being in a lower weight class is you don't have to wait very long to wrestle. I was chomping at the bits to get my match under-way. I was like a racehorse, eagerly awaiting its release from the starting gate. I just knew that, whoever my opponent was, was going to be in for the fight of his life!

I raced to the head table to check in, bolted out onto the mat, and stared knives into my opponent. With my heart pounding and my body poised for attack, I anxiously awaited the ref's blowing his whistle to begin the match. The whistle sounded, and my opponent and I began to circle one another. We locked up, and it was as if I locked up with a bear. I tried to execute my double leg takedown but to no avail. With one mighty push, my adversary had me off my feet and flat on my back. Luckily, I had the where-with-al to bridge onto my stomach. Soon after, I felt the weight of my foe on top of me as the air was forced out of my lungs.

I began to feel his hand creep underneath my shoulder and onto the back of my neck. Even though my wrestling career was in its infancy, this move was quickly becoming the bane of my existence. It was called the half nelson. A move so simple, it is the first pinning combination you learn as a novice wrestler. Yet, I have seen some of the most experienced wrestlers get caught up in its grasp if they weren't careful.

"Look away and peel the hand off!" Coach Landau yelled.

I managed to fight off his first few attempts to try to flip me over, but inevitably, my arms began to grow tired, and my opponent flipped me onto my back. I desperately tried to fight off my back as the ref was making the five-count, but my body was too fatigued. The next sound I heard was the resounding smack of the referee's hand meeting the mat and him blowing his whistle, signaling the match was over. I once again had to look across the mat at my opponent as he was getting his hand raised in victory. I didn't even make it past the first period. I obviously wasn't the best technician.

As I was walking off the mat, my coaches and a number of my teammates began to counsel me, telling me what a great job I did. I appreciated all of the kind words, but the competitor in me knew I had to be capable of more. I cheered on my fellow teammates as they competed in their matches. They made it look so easy, specifically Dominic, D.J. and Micah. Their movements were so fluid and precise: they executed moves with the greatest of ease.

I can't wait to get on their level someday.

Before I knew it, it was time for my second match of the day. I was just as determined as ever; I was going to give this next kid the fight of his life. Some may have called my level of confidence annoying.

You may be thinking: *How could you say such a thing when you get your butt kicked all the time?*

I'm not sure of many things, but I'm sure of one thing. If you go through life thinking you're going to fail, you've already failed.

I made my way to the wrestling mat, and I realized I was wrestling against somebody from a school I didn't recognize. As I stepped on the mat, nerves began to swell inside of me. All of a sudden, without warning, it seemed, the ref blew the whistle, and the match had begun. Still shrouded in a cloud of nervousness, I was quickly brought back to reality when my opponent took me down with such force that the room began to spin. I quickly bridged on my neck and returned to my belly. As soon as I thought I was safe, I began to feel the all too familiar sensation of my opponent trying to sink in the half nelson.

Not this time!

I raised my head up as much as I could and pried his hand away from my neck. Frustrated, he applied more force to the half nelson and attempted to roll me over by ramming his head into my rib cage. Painfully aware of the impending danger I was in, I flexed my core and planted my arm as hard as I could. I was like a rock; steadfast and immovable. I could sense his frustration growing, as my opponent desperately tried to put me on my back but to no avail. This exchange went on for about 45 seconds until the ref blew the whistle and called for the second period.

I actually made it past the first period! I was so proud of myself, but I knew the real objective was to win the match. The ref pulled out a two-sided coin with the colors red and green on it. Whichever color the coin lands on when it is flipped, the person wearing that colored ankle bracelet gets to pick the position they want. Either on top in the referee's position, on bottom in the referee's position, or in neutral, how you start the match.

The coin landed on red, which just so happened to be the color of my ankle bracelet. I glanced at my coaches for guidance, and they suggested I choose bottom. I got into position and I awaited my opponent to mount. The wait for the ref to blow the whistle while in the referee's position was agonizing. What was only a few seconds felt like an eternity.

Finally, the ref gave the signal, and we began to do battle once again. I remembered what DJ told me to do, and I began to imitate what I had done in practice. Just as I was preparing to launch myself forward, a hand reached between my right leg, and another hand was reaching over my left shoulder. The two hands connected with one another and, before I knew it, I was falling backward against my will. I was caught in a cradle. I flailed and kicked but it was no use. I was trapped in my opponent's vice-like grip. I was so focused on breaking the grip, that I didn't even hear the referee counting. Only when he hit the mat, did I know the match was over. I had lost again. Tired and out of breath, I shook my opponent's hand and watched him get his arm raised. I obviously wasn't in the best of shape.

Even though I lost, I was still proud of my performance. I sat down on the bleachers and looked up at the balcony. As I looked, I noticed that not only were my parents present but my cousin Hunter was too. Then I spotted my occupational therapist, Jane, and my physical therapist, Jada. It felt good to have so much support, even when you lose.

In wrestling, you will find it is a very fast-paced sport. Just when you get done using the bathroom and grabbing a quick drink, you have another match on the horizon. This was going to be my final match of the day, and I wanted to make it count. Especially since it was against Circleville. I was bound and determined to go all three rounds with this guy.

We stepped onto the mat and glared at each other with malicious intent. We got into our stances and the ref blew the whistle. Like all of my previous matches, my opponent got the first offensive move of the exchange and went straight for the half nelson. I fought it off as he rolled me over onto my back. The ref began to count but I flipped back over on my belly before he was able to get to five.

We were back to square one. He tried to sink in the half nelson again, but I fought it off. Our intense squabble was interrupted by the referee's whistle, which signaled the end of the first period. My opponent was selected to pick, and he chose bottom, which meant I was on top. I mounted onto my opponent, and the ref blew the whistle. I snatched his ankle to bring him down to his belly, but unfortunately, he wiggled free. Back on our feet, he lunged toward me, taking me down with the greatest of ease.

I found myself once again fighting to get off my back, which I was able to do successfully. Each time I would get back onto my belly, he would respond with another half nelson and another head in the rib cage. After what seemed like hours, the ref blew the whistle to end the second period. I had made it to the third period, but my body was so fatigued from fighting off the onslaught of attempted pin falls that I could barely move.

I dragged my worn-out body over to the center of the mat and took the bottom position. My opponent mounted, and the ref blew the whistle. I found myself experiencing déjà vu from my last match because my opponent quickly locked me into a cradle. I began to kick like a wild bull, and, miraculously, I was able to break free. That was followed up, however, by a half nelson into yet another pinning predicament. Using every last bit of my strength, I bridged on my neck and dug my heels into the mat and began to inch ever so slowly to the edge of the mat, where I was successful in breaking the pin.

I stood up and looked at the clock--only ten seconds remained. If I could last just ten more seconds, then I would have lasted all three rounds. The ref blew the whistle, and my opponent took me down yet again. He tried to put in the half nelson, but I managed to fight it off. The whistle blew, the match was over, but I did what I had set out to do. I went to shake my opponent's hand and noticed he had beads of sweat rolling down his face. I had given him the fight of his life!

I put my clothes on and very slowly and carefully made my way up to the balcony. I got halfway up the stairs and was met by my mom.

"Good job, Bubba!" she exclaimed. I could only manage a weak smile.

After the meet was over, Coach Landau called us over for a team break before we left.

"Great job today, guys," Coach Landau said. "You guys wrestled good! Now let's get ready for the next one."

We all raised our hands into the center of the circle, and DJ cried out, "No guts, no glory, on 3!"

"1, 2, 3, no guts no glory!" we all shouted in unison.

As we were walking out of the building, Coach McComas tapped me on the shoulder.

"You know, Trev," Coach McComas said, "you've got more heart than anyone on this team."

I smiled from ear to ear as we boarded the bus.

Beyond the Mat

Early in my wrestling career, I pictured myself being the best wrestler in Logan Elm's history and surpassing all the greats. When I found out that I had trouble beating even the worst of the junior varsity, I attributed it to a lack of experience. My goal as the season progressed was to be as good as DJ or Dominic. As the season progressed, though, the only thing that progressed was my discouragement. Why? Because I was comparing my progress to their already established skill and continued progress.

Having cerebral palsy, I've always met certain milestones slower than my peers. It never bothered me when running with my friends at recess, but I let it bother me in the midst of the competitiveness of wrestling. I beat myself up when I wasn't winning like the rest of my teammates. 1 Corinthians 10:12 says, "We dare not class ourselves and compare ourselves with those who commend themselves..." (NKJV). Do not compare yourself with someone else; you'll always disappoint yourself.

Coach McComas' comment let me know that, despite all of my losses, I was still a valuable member of the team who possessed a quality that no one else on the team had. You are created with your own unique fingerprint. There is no one else like you in the universe.

You might not be the best football player, wrestler, or preacher. However, there is a quality inside you that God wants to use to bless those around you. You don't have to be the next Tom Brady, the next Dan Gable, or the next Billy Graham to make an impact. Just be you.

4

The Streak

February 2011

"Therefore, since we have this ministry, as we have received mercy, we do not lose heart."

2 Corinthians 4:1 (NKJV)

The final bell of the school day rang, and I made my way out to the wrestling barn. It was late February, and the season was quickly winding down. It was the final practice before the final meet of the season, and I couldn't help but reflect on how well my first season went.

In the beginning, I was worried that everybody was going to make fun of me and not take me seriously. To my surprise, quite the opposite happened. I couldn't have asked for better teammates and coaches. Instead of getting frustrated when I couldn't perform a certain move, they would work with me and help me adapt to see if there was another way I could do the move. They knew I had a disability, but they still treated me like one of the boys. This includes not going easy on me in practice and pulling relentless pranks. Don't worry, it was all in good fun. I pulled my fair share of pranks as well.

I have to say, during this time I managed to accomplish quite an accolade. I dare say it rivals The Undertakers 21-0 winning streak at WrestleMania. During my first tenure in the beloved sport of wrestling, I had an unprecedented record of 0-33! It takes a lot of work to build up that kind of resumé in such a short time.

Upon entering the locker room, I was greeted by my fellow teammates. I got dressed and began to warm up. We completed our ten-minute warm-up jog, which surprisingly had gotten a little easier from the beginning of the season despite my increased energy expenditure. Since it was the last practice of the season, we didn't work on anything new. Instead, we critiqued what we already knew. Everybody loved the practices the day before a meet because we knew that it was going to be an easy day with lots of trash can basketball!

We ended the practice with a round of conditioning. Coach Landau left Dustin White in charge of the end of conditioning. I always hated when Dustin led conditioning because he always made us do mat drills, or grass drills, as they call them in football. To perform the exercise, you start by running in place, taking short, explosive steps. Then when the leader yells, "Hit it!", you sprawl to the mat and return to your feet as fast as you can.

"Get 'em choppin'!" Dustin yelled.

I ran in place as fast as my legs would allow me. It seemed like an eternity before Dustin's voice echoed through the wrestling barn.

"Hit it!" We sounded like a herd of elephants wandering through the safari as our bodies all met that mat at the same time. Within a millisecond it seemed, everyone was back on their feet, everyone except me. I had no problem keeping up with everyone on the first mat drill, it was the second, the third, the fourth where I lagged behind. My brain would not allow me to get up as fast as I wanted, and it grew worse as I fatigued. As a result, I was always the last one who would finish their mat drill.

Once practice was over, we all piled into the small locker room. Cerebral palsy makes it very difficult to maneuver in small or crowded spaces. This struggle, combined with post- practice gossip, guarantees that I am going to spend at least 15-20 minutes getting dressed. After getting dressed, I walked out and overheard my dad and Coach Landau talking.

"Yeah, he's a really hard worker," Coach Landau bragged, "We just need to perfect his skill set."

Being the curious person that I am, I decided to join in on the conversation.

Coach Landau smiled at me. "We're going to get you a win one of these days," he said.

"Yeah," I said with a hint of uncertainty.

"We will," he assured with a smile.

Last Chance

The bell finally sounded for the end of the school day, and I made my way to the wrestling room. It was nearing the end of the regular season and the beginning of the Mid State League championships. MSL meets are always held in the middle of the week, which makes it difficult to prepare for if you are inexperienced. This was our last meet of the season and, it was my last chance of the year to win a match. It was a tri-meet, which meant there were only going to be three teams at the meet: I only had two more chances to win a match, I had to make them count.

The cool thing about a tri-meet was that the high school team was wrestling at the meet also. I was going to be wrestling alongside my cousin BJ. I couldn't wait to show him what I could do. When we arrived, we barely had time to put our stuff down before the officials rushed us back to get weighed in. The worst travesty of all, we hardly had time to eat! To a wrestler, the consumption of food is a sacred time. That first drop of Gatorade right after weigh-ins is like medicine for the soul.

It never ceases to amaze me how fast time seems to pass when preparing for a wrestling match. You want your match to come fast to get it over with, but at the same time, you want more time to try to ease your nerves. I sat down in one of the chairs situated on the edge of the mat. I liked the set up of MSL meets. We all sit around the perimeter of the mat, and we get to watch all the matches that take place. That can be both a blessing and a curse.

Before long, it was time for the first match of the night. Thankfully, for this kind of meet, we were going by order of weight class. We started with 86lbs, which was Justin's weight class. Coach Landau instructed we send Justin out. We all laid hands on Justin and shouted in unison, "No guts, no glory!" I was amazed at the amount of skill Justin possessed. He made short work of his opponent, pinning him in just shy of thirty seconds. It was amazing how easy he made winning look.

It wasn't long before I had my chance at victory. My teammates laid hands on me and shouted in unison, "No guts, no glory!" I made my way over to the head table and made eye contact with my opponent. He was a tall, lanky kid. I hated wrestling tall, lanky kids because my short arms could only stretch so far to accommodate their elongated frame. Coincidentally, that was precisely what my downfall was in this particular match.

We made our way out to the mat and eagerly awaited the referee's signal to begin the match. The ref's whistle blew, and I immediately dove for the leg. I got what I wanted: I had his leg in my grasp. But it was just as I feared, he sprawled out, and I quickly began to lose my grip. With my triceps muscle being painfully stretched and my shoulder threatening to dislocate, I had no choice but to let go. As soon as I did, he spun around me and scored a takedown.

From there, he locked in a half chicken wing and slowly began to turn me onto my back. The angle he was at allowed him to jam the bony prominence of his elbow directly into my sternum. Struggling to breathe, I tried desperately to get back onto my belly, but I couldn't escape before the referee ended the match with an emphatic slap of the mat. I had lost yet again and in the first period.

I was disappointed by the loss, but I knew I had one more chance to add a win to my record. After a short break, it was time to wrestle the other team. I was really enjoying the atmosphere of the MSL meets. The screams and cheers from teammates as they watched their brothers go to war with an adversary, blended with the love, support, and correction from teammates after a win or loss. It was the first time I really got a glimpse of the brotherhood that the sport of wrestling embodies. It is unique, unlike any other sport in the world.

Being engrossed by the action, I had almost forgotten I had a match coming up until my brothers were laying their hands on my head. This was my last chance for the year, a shot at redemption I would never get back, and I was determined to make it count. I glanced over at the opposing mat where the high schoolers were wrestling just in time to see BJ pick up and body slam a 285-lb. behemoth. I'm not sure why, but for some reason, that motivated me even more to get the win!

More determined than ever, I looked my opponent dead in the eyes: this means war! As soon as the whistle blew, I attacked his leg. As I struggled to get to my knees, I was met with a forearm across the nose. In a daze, I attempted to get back to my feet but to no avail. Using the momentum of this barbaric blow, he flipped me onto my back. Once in this vulnerable position, he added insult to injury by pinning my legs against his so that I couldn't move or bridge. Inevitably, I lost the match.

I walked off the mat and was immediately embraced with hugs and handshakes by my teammates.

"Great season, Trev," Coach Landau said. "I really enjoyed having you on the team this year."

"Thanks," I said, smiling from ear to ear.

I finished my first season with a record of 0-35. While I would have liked to have won at least one match this year and finish the season in somewhat of a climactic fashion, that does not compare to the friends and memories I made. Needless to say, I made a decision that I was definitely wrestling again next year. Who knows? Maybe I'll finally get my first win. I can't quit when I'm one match away from victory!

8th Grade
2011-2012

5

The Birth of the Crossface

September 2011

"Not that I speak from want, for I have learned to be content in whatever circumstances I am. I know how to get along with humble means, and I also know how to live in prosperity; in any and every circumstance I have learned the secret of being filled and going hungry, both of having abundance and suffering need."

Philippians 4:11 – 12 (NASB)

The summer came and went in the blink of an eye and before I knew it, it was time to go back to school. I had been in school a month before it was finally time for open mats to begin. What excited me the most was the fact that almost everyone who wrestled from the year before was coming back again this year! However, my nerves couldn't help but simmer at the thought of the 7th graders that were going to be joining the team this year. Would they accept me just as the previous group of boys did?

After school, I headed out to the wrestling barn. It felt good to be able to get back onto the mat again after being off for so long. I walked into the wrestling barn and noticed that it still had that same musty smell that I had grown to love. I advanced further into the locker room and noticed that Justin had gotten here before me. He no longer had his Justin Bieber haircut. Instead, he wore it shorter with a hint of hair gel in the front.

"Hey, Trev!" Justin said.

"What's up?" I asked as we shook hands.

We continued to exchange conversation as I stepped on the scale. To my surprise, it said 108lbs. I had worked out and trained all summer and I was only able to gain 4 pounds.

"Somebody has gotten fat," Justin joked.

To my delight, Coach Polly who was one of the high school coaches, was there to greet me. Coach Polly is a tall, skinny man with a rapidly receding hairline. He wore a t-shirt, a pair of shorts, and a Logan Elm baseball cap.

"What's up, Coach Polly?" I asked.

"How's it going, Trev?" Coach Polly returned, "I'm here to make sure nobody gets hurt," he said sarcastically.

I looked around the room and noticed that there weren't very many kids to look after. Justin and I seemed to be the only two kids to have shown up.

"That's okay, Trev," Justin reassured. "We'll just wrestle each other."

I ecstatically obliged. I was eager to see how much stronger I had gotten and how that would help me with my technique. We started out taking turns drilling takedowns. Unsurprisingly, I was still unsteady on my feet but that didn't bother me as much as it used to. Then it was my turn. I dove for Justin's legs to set up my favorite takedown, the double leg. I successfully penetrated his base but as I was getting ready to lift him up and complete the move, my back suddenly gave out and I ended up falling to the floor.

"Let's try that again," I laughed.

I regained my bearings and tried again. I repeated the steps that I had done before, I began to feel the weight of Justin's body shift into my arms as his feet left the ground. Seconds later, I had successfully completed a double leg takedown. With a smile on his face, Justin leaped to his feet and lunged toward me like a hungry lion. This unprovoked attack caused me to fall flat on my back. Realizing the predicament I was in, I quickly bridged on my neck and squirmed my way out of Justin's grasp.

He wasn't finished with me yet, however. On my stomach, desperately trying to get back to my base, I began to feel the all-too-familiar sensation of a hand clutching the back of my neck. The Half Nelson was quickly becoming the bane of my existence. Soon after, I began to feel Justin's head press into my ribcage. I knew what was coming next; he was going to try to pin me! I posted on my arm as hard as I could in order to prevent that from happening. Try as he might, as Justin pushed against me, my body was moving but I was not budging.

Justin looked up at me with a tired smile, "Still as strong as ever, I see."

"Yep," I smiled back. "Let's work on referee's position," I suggested.

In agreement, Justin assumed the bottom referee's position. I mounted onto Justin and he began to hit the mat three times which was the signal to start. Once his hand hit the mat for the third time, before Justin could react, I cocked my right arm back and cross-faced him as hard as I could. A sickening smack could be heard as my forearm made contact with his orbital bone.

"Ow!" Justin yelled in pain. "I can't see!"

"Are you okay?" I said holding back laughter.

Justin uncovered his face revealing a red, swollen, watery eye.

"He got you good, Justin," Coach Polly said laughing.

"I can't wait to show Coach Landau what I can do," I said.

Coach Polly seemed surprised, "You haven't heard?"

"Heard what?" I asked curiously.

Coach Polly blurted, "The junior high is getting a new coach this year."

6

There's a New Sheriff in Town

November 2011

For we wrestle not against flesh and blood, but against principalities, against powers, against the rulers of the darkness of this world, against spiritual wickedness in high places.

Ephesians 6:12 (KJV)

The news shook me to the core. I couldn't believe we were getting a new coach. I felt like I was just getting to know Coach Landau and Coach McComas. One day, while walking to class, I crossed paths with Coach Barnes. I figured if anyone would knew the identity of the new coach, it would be him.

"Hey, Coach Barnes," I said.

"Hey, champ," he replied with a smile. "Are you ready for practice to start?"

"You know it!" "Speaking of which, you wouldn't happen to know who the new junior high wrestling coach is, would you?"

He looked up from tying his shoe and met my gaze. "Coach Bennett," he rattled off.

"What time is practice going to be?" I asked, changing the subject.

"Right after school," Coach Barnes said. "The junior high and the high school are going to be practicing together this year," he added. "We're going to be one big, happy family."

That's exciting. I'll get to practice with D.J, Dominick, and all the others I wrestled with last year.

I walked to class, pondering what the new coach was going to be like. Was he tall or short? Was he going to be calm and laid back like Coach Landau or as tough and mean as a drill sergeant?

Meeting the man

I walked into the wrestling barn and headed straight for the locker room, and already, I ran across a new face. This kid was so skinny, he appeared to be two-dimensional. I was afraid he was going to get mauled by even the smallest of competitors.

"Hello there," I said awkwardly. "What's your name?"

"Chase," he responded.

Amongst the commotion as people began filing in, Troy walked in along with another new face I had never seen before, yet he looked so familiar.

"Who's that?" I asked out of curiosity.

"That's Nick Vagnier," Troy answered. "He's Dominick Vagnier's brother."

Suddenly, it all made sense. I then came to the realization I was going to be in serious trouble if Nick was as good as Dom. I quickly came to my senses and realized I had to quit thinking like that. Anybody could be beaten on any given day, no matter what sort of physical condition they were in. I walked outside, and I was instructed by a short, stocky man with brown hair and a freckled complexion, to join the rest of my teammates on the floor.

"My name is Coach Bennett," he began. "I am the new junior high coach. I want to start off by laying some ground rules," he paused. "There will be no cursing or any kind of dirty language. We are a team, and we aren't going to call anybody names or degrade anyone for any reason." He scanned the room to make sure we got the message. "We are a team, we are to love one another," Coach Bennett continued. "That's the principle on which I live by, that is the standard of God's Word."

God's Word? I believe in God and all that, but save that kind of stuff for church.

After he went over the ground rules, Coach Bennett dismissed us to begin our warm-up jog. Just like the previous year, the clock was set for ten minutes and around the room we went. I may have gotten stronger over the summer, but I quickly realized that my cardio conditioning had suffered. Not even five minutes in and my lungs were already burning and gasping for air. This internal struggle turned my already slow jog, into a snail-paced marathon run, but I was determined to finish strong.

Finally, the whining of the timer signaled the end of the jog and we began our active stretching. At this time the previous year, I could hardly do anything the other kids were doing because I would lose my balance and fall. I was hoping the training I did over the summer improved my balance, even by the little slightest bit.

"Shots!" Micah called out.

We all formed our lines and, one by one began to shoot from one end of the building to the other. Finally, it was my turn. I carefully stepped forward with my stronger right leg and slowly began to lower myself into a stance to swing my left leg through. Once my left knee touched the mat, however, I began to topple over and fell to the ground. Not one to be defeated so easily, I decided to get up and try again and again and again. Each time I tried, I met the ground more quickly than the first time. Inevitably, I swallowed my pride and ran down to the other end as to not hold up everyone else.

I had a chance to redeem myself, though, because we did the same exercise on the way back to the other side. Although it didn't matter which side of the building I was on, because the result was the same. Coach Bennett must have seen my frustration, because he walked toward me and with the most compassionate smile I've ever seen someone give, said, "I know you've got a bum leg, just do the best you can." His reassurance broadened my confidence and quieted my nerves.

After warm-ups, Coach Bennett called us into a circle. He showed us all of the basics since it was the first day of practice, and then dismissed us to drill with a partner. As luck would have it, I got partnered up with Chase.

"You can go first," Chase said.

We locked up, and I quickly shot in for a double leg. When I hoisted him up, it was just as I suspected; he was as light as a feather. Trouble is, I still had difficulty controlling how hard or how fast my opponent hit the mat. As quickly as I picked Chase up, I dropped him onto the mat with a resounding thud. Visibly shaken, Chase rose to his feet and shot in for a single leg. The force of his attack was magnified, as I felt the boney landmark of his shoulder digging into my thigh. The velocity alone was enough to send my flying backward flat onto my back.

It was my turn again, and of course, I went for my bread and butter. I set up the double leg like normal, except this time when I shot in, I was unable to lift Chase up, and I fell on my side. Coach Bennett walked over and offered a suggestion I hadn't even thought of.

"Try wrestling on your knees," he said. "You'll have a much more solid base than if you were standing."

Coach Bennett sent Chase off to work with somebody else so that he could help me perfect this new technique. He gave me the signal to start, and I dropped to my knees. As soon as I did, he put his hands in my face blocking my view.

"Smack my hands away," he instructed.

I did as he said, and that opened up my view of his legs. I quickly dove in and wrapped my arms as tightly as I could around him. With one swift motion, I pulled his legs in closer to my body, and he crumbled to the floor. I had successfully completed the move.

"You could win the first match of your career, if you would just learn to wrestle on your knees," Coach Bennett said, smiling from ear to ear. Little did I know, I would be fighting a lot of battles on my knees.

"Now, let's work on referee's position." He called Chase back over and instructed me to get on my hands and knees. "I've noticed you've had trouble with getting into the half really easy," Coach Bennett said. "I'm going to teach you how to bunny hop so you can stay on your base. Lay on your stomach," he instructed. "When Chase is on top of you, I want you to bring your knees up underneath you."

I did as I was told, and I brought my knees up underneath me. To my surprise, it worked! I was able to get back to my base more efficiently than trying to struggle not to get pinned the entire match. After I had practiced the bunny hop a few times, Coach Bennett helped me work on moves that could help me get back on the offensive. Coach Bennett was so patient with me, he really did want me to succeed. Maybe this new coach won't be so bad after all.

Righteous Anger Ignited - *The next day*

In the hectic environment that is wrestling practice, you tend to not pay attention to anything other than what's going on in front of you. That was the case for me, at least. I had completely disregarded the high schoolers being in the room with us until I learned that we were going to partake in a conditioning exercise together.

We went about our normal routine. We completed our jog, warm-up exercises and waited for Coach Bennett to give further instruction.

"Everybody grab a weight plate." Coach Bennett said.

I went over to explore my options. I saw a 45lb plate and thought that surely, I would be strong enough to handle it. I pulled it off the rack and brought it to my chest. I quickly found out that lifting it wasn't the problem, it was carrying the weight. Every time I took a step, the threat arose that I might lose my balance. As a result, I was forced to resort to using the 25lb plate instead.

As we all gathered around in a circle, Coach Bennett began to demonstrate our first exercise.

"Halo's," Coach Bennett called out.

He lifted the weight above his head and began to make a circular motion with the weight plate. We all began to mimic what he was doing. I lifted the weight above my head and attempted to do the exercise. I found that when I tried to make the circular motion, I would lose my balance.

"Steering wheels!" Coach Bennett yelled out.

He held the weight straight out in front of him and began to turn it as if he were driving a car. I did the same and I quickly began to feel a burning sensation in my arms. After about 30 seconds, my arms began screaming for relief. After what seemed like an eternity, Coach Bennett called out the next exercise.

"Diamond push-ups," Coach Bennett bellowed.

Coach Bennett set his plate on the ground and placed his hands around the center to form a diamond-like shape. As he did this, he began doing push-ups. Once again, we mimicked what he was doing, and I found this exercise to be quite easy thanks to my improved upper body strength. We did several more exercises on the floor. After a while, it was apparent everyone myself included, was getting tired.

"Come on," Coach Bennett yelled. "This is bullcrap! When you come into this gym, I expect you to give it everything you've got and not go halfway!" His voice echoed throughout the building, and his eyes seethed with rage. "We're going to do this whole circuit over again and do it right this time!"

True to his word, we did the entire circuit over again from start to finish but Coach Bennett wasn't finished just yet.

"Get into a push-up position and hold it," Coach Bennett said. "Let's see who can hold it the longest," he challenged.

Many people gave up as their arms were too fatigued to hold them up. I looked around the room and discovered that I was the only junior high kid who was still in the contest. Only three people remained — Dominick, D.J, and myself.

"Yeah Trevor! Yeah Trevor! Yeah!" Coach Bennett screamed.

My arms began to feel like jelly, and I could feel I was on the verge of collapsing.

"Don't you dare give up on me, dawg." BJ encouraged.

After seven agonizing minutes, all three of us who remained collapsed to the floor with Dominick being the victor. After the circuit, Coach Bennett summoned us into a huddle.

"Sometimes it's not all about strength," Coach Bennett began. "Sometimes, it's about heart and your willingness to never give up."

It was then I realized Coach Bennett did all of that not as a punishment but to teach us all a valuable lesson. Hard work and guts beats talent any day. Maybe he wasn't going to be such a bad coach after all.

Beyond the Mat

Proverbs 3:12 – 13 says, "My son, do not despise the chastening of the Lord, Nor detest His correction; For whom the Lord loves He corrects, Just as a father the son in whom he delights. There may be times in your life where you're going through a rough patch, and you can't understand why. In the same way that Coach Bennett made us do those extra workouts, God may put some roadblocks in your path or trouble your spirit to correct you. Not necessarily as punishment but to refine you and make you stronger. You don't get better by sitting on the couch, and you don't grow your relationship with God by simply going through the motions.

7

Déjà Vu

December 2011

Consider it all joy, my brethren, when you encounter various trials, knowing that the testing of your faith produces endurance. And let endurance have its perfect result, so that you may be perfect and complete, lacking in nothing.

James 1:2 – 4 (NASB)

Two weeks of practice flew by in an instant and, before I knew it, it was time for the first meet of the season. Fortunately for me, there was nobody else on the team that was in the 110 lb. weight class. That meant I didn't have to wrestle anybody for the position, and automatically obtained the varsity spot. I was excited to start the season off varsity, but, deep down, I was hoping I wouldn't have to wrestle anybody for the position.

The location for our first meet seemed a bit strange to me. We were going to be hosting the match, but it wasn't going to be held in the gym — it was going to be held in the building where we practice. As people began to file in, it was just as I suspected. The room began to feel like we were compacted in a can of sardines, and the spectators hadn't even arrived yet. Coach Bennett frantically got everybody weighed in, and it was time to warm up.

It's going to be interesting to see how the new guys do.

As more and more people began to cram themselves in, it began to feel like someone cranked up the heat in the Logan Elm athletic complex. It was so hot, sweat began to pour off my body before my match had even started. Our first match of the night, however, was a new, first-year 172-pound wrestler named Vince. Both combatants stepped onto the mat, and the whistle sounded. Immediately, Vince locked up and took his opponent down to the mat. In a flash, he locked in the half nelson and had his opponent flat on his back. Try as he might to break free, it was a lost cause. Vince secured his victory in dominating fashion, and in thirty seconds, no less.

Next up was Thomas, and, as expected, he finished off his opponent without hardly even breaking a sweat. While Thomas and I were best friends, I wasn't about to let him upstage me. Finally, after watching some of my fellow teammates triumph in victory or experience the sting of defeat, it was my turn. I stepped onto the mat and was bombarded with the screams and cheers of spectators. With so many people packed so tightly in such a small space, the noise was almost deafening. I couldn't let that deter my focus, though— I was about to go to war! The whistle sounded, and we locked horns. We came at each other with such force that I fell backward onto my back.

Realizing I was not in a good place, I quickly rolled onto my belly. I was about to stand back up when, suddenly, my opponent was right back on top of me.

"Bunny hop! Bunny hop!" Coach Bennett screamed.

Try as I might, even though I wanted to do what the coach was telling me, my body simply would not do what I wanted it to. With cerebral palsy, your body is literally not in sync with itself. The brain sends the wrong signals to the muscles. As a result, the muscle either misfires and causes a muscle spasm or doesn't do anything at all when you want it to. In my case, at that moment, my body wasn't doing anything I was telling it to do. I fought him off for as long as I could, but eventually, my opponent did get the pin-fall. Even still, I walked off the mat with a smile on my face. I was just happy to get back on the mat again.

As I was putting my clothes back on, one of the new additions of the team, Kyle, sat down beside me.

"That was awesome, Trev," Kyle said. "You should have seen the look on that kid's face when he couldn't roll you over the first time he tried. It was priceless."

"Thanks," I said.

I watched my other teammates compete in their matches, and, at the end of the day, we ended up winning the dual. Tiffany, my physical therapist from school, surprised me by coming to watch. All in all, it was a great start to the season.

So Close

Our next meet was at Paint Valley Middle School, and I was bound and determined to get that first win. Once we arrived, I joined my teammates on the bleachers while we waited for the event to get started. There is nothing that compares to the anticipation of waiting to receive your bout number. On the one hand, you would like to have a bigger number, so you would have more time to prepare, but at the same time you want a smaller number, so you can hurry up and get the first match out of the way. Coach Bennett came out of the coach's room to give everybody their numbers. I was given number 34.

"You have a bye the first round," Coach Bennett said. That meant I would have to wait until next round to wrestle. I sat and watched intently as the first matches of the day started. Justin, who was sitting a couple of rows below me, turned around and spoke up.

"Hey, Trev," he said, "There's the first kid you're going to have to wrestle. I think you can beat him," Justin said, confidently.

The kid was wearing a solid red singlet and was rather short in stature and pudgy. To make matters worse, he didn't look a day past ten. Surely, I would be able to beat him. I watched as both wrestlers took their places on the mat, and the match began. Both competitors locked up, and my future opponent grabbed his adversary by the waist and hoisted him over his hip, which caused him to splatter onto the mat with a thud. Keeping ahold of his victim's arm, he squeezed with all of his might until the poor child's face turned a crimson red. Ultimately, the kid I thought I could get a win over won the match mere seconds after it began. Justin cackled in laughter as my jaw hit the floor, and my eyes doubled in size.

I guess I should have known better, not to judge a book by its cover, I thought.

Before I knew it, it was time for the next round and time for my first match of the day. Justin was right, the kid I just saw mop the floor with another kid was my first opponent. Needless to say, I was nervous. We took our positions, shook hands, and the ref blew the whistle. We locked up, and, while I knew I would be able to overpower him, he proceeded to grab my leg, and instantly, my body folded, and I collapsed to the ground.

He wasn't going to get one over on me that easily. I could sense that he was trying to do what so many others before him had succeeded in, lock in the half nelson, and plant me on my back. By this time, I had gotten pretty familiar with the technique, so I grabbed his hand and tucked it underneath me so neither he nor I could move.

Unfortunately, since neither of us could move, the referee said I was stalling and gave me a warning. My opponent quickly jumped to the other side and locked in the half nelson, but before he could roll me over, the buzzer sounded for the end of the first period. I made my way over to the center of the mat as the ref flipped the coin. It landed on red, which meant I would have the option to choose what position I wanted.

I chose top because I knew that I wouldn't be fast enough to get an escape, so my best bet was to catch him in cradle. We mounted our positions, and the ref blew the whistle. Before I could react, he was already behind me and had scored a reversal. I was back to square one, fighting off half nelsons and pin attempts for the entire second period.

Fortunately, I was able to survive his onslaught yet again, but it was not without cost. The constant struggle of having to use every ounce of energy just to stay in the match had taken its toll. I slowly crawled over to the center circle and could barely support the weight of my opponent as we waited for the signal to begin. My entire body was trembling with exhaustion. The ref blew the whistle, and my opponent picked up my left ankle and drove me flat on my stomach. Even in my fatigued state, I was determined not to get pinned. I felt him trying to sink the half. At that moment, I miraculously found the strength to bring my knees up to my chest and push myself back up onto my hands and knees.

Aware that I wasn't out of the woods, I slowly brought my right leg forward to attempt a stand-up. Before I knew it, I was falling backward into yet another pinning predicament! My opponent used the opening I had created to lock in a cradle. I flailed and kicked like a madman, frantically trying to break his vise-like grip. I was successful, but a mere second later, he locked it in again. I found myself flailing and kicking once again, but this time his grip was not budging.

I was left with no other choice but to break his grip with my fatigued, shaking hands. All the while, I had to be aware of the referee's piercing gaze on my shoulders. At this point, if they graze the mat even once, it's over. Keeping my shoulder blades retracted, I began to pry at his grip. With no success, I decided to interject my right leg into the occasion by pushing on his arm. I pushed and pulled with everything I had until finally, I broke free from his grasp. I gazed at the clock, only ten seconds remained. Surely, I can last another ten seconds. My opponent capitalized on my momentary distraction and locked in the half yet again. I fought with all my might in what was the longest ten seconds of my life. In the end, I may have lost the match, but I didn't get pinned.

Beaten and exhausted, I walked off the mat and melted into the floor behind the bleachers. As I sat trying to catch my breath, my opponent walked over, breathless himself.

"That was a great match," he said.

"Thanks," I said, in between gasps. There was a long pause for a moment before he finally spoke up.

"Did I hurt you?" he asked.

"What? No," I said, surprised.

"Good," he said relieved. "I didn't want to hurt your legs."

I sensed the sympathy in his voice. "I wouldn't have gotten into this sport if I was scared of the possibility of getting hurt," I said. "Every time I step out onto the map, treat me like one of the boys," I smiled.

"Oh, I did!" he insisted. "I had to. You're as strong as an ox!"

"Good," I said. "I would expect nothing less."

We shook hands, and I watched him walk away. As always, my mom was there to congratulate me after a hard-fought match. As I was gulping down my lemon-lime Gatorade, I came to the stunning realization I still had one more match for the night. I slowly stood up, still shaking, and I could feel the lactic acid begin to build up in my already–tight muscles.

Sometime later, I saw my bout number appear on the screen yet again. I eagerly made my way over to the mat and awaited the arrival of my opponent. I was already in the center circle when he arrived. He was my height and just a bit skinnier than me. The ref blew the whistle, and it was on. I immediately attacked his leg and held on for dear life.

Try as he might, he just couldn't break my iron grip. I knew I needed to get on my knees to fully execute the takedown, but my body wouldn't allow it. If I used my stronger arm to assist me, he would break free for sure. As I struggled to pick myself up, the buzzer sounded. Had we really stayed like that for the whole period?

I received the option of choosing the position. The ref blew the whistle, and I nailed my opponent with a cross face. He ducked underneath my attack, grabbed my leg, and locked in the half. I felt myself being lifted off the ground and landed flat on my back. I heard the ref begin his count as I fought to get off my back. I avoided the pin fall, but I had a long way to go to get back on my feet. For the rest of the period, I continued to fight off pin attempt after pin attempt until finally, the buzzer sounded once more.

At this point, my reserves of strength were depleted. I had no choice but to rely on sheer willpower to finish the match. Since I got to be on top in the referee's position during the second period, I was on the bottom position by default for the third period. Fighting the ache of my trembling extremities, I stood up as hard and as fast as I could to break free from my opponent's grasp. I was successful but immediately fell to the ground. Still on my knees, I feverishly locked up with him in a last–ditched effort to score and possibly get a pin fall. As I tried desperately to reach for his leg, he began to push me backward. He pushed me back until I was sitting on my ankles and then pushed me even further.

Because of my cerebral palsy, some of my joints dislocate easily. I could feel my hip begin to dislodge from its socket and knew I had to act quickly. I had no choice but to allow him to get a takedown and work from there. He got the takedown and locked in the half. There were only thirty seconds left in the match. I had to act fast. I ripped his hand off of my neck and torqued his arm as hard as I could. I felt the weight of my opponent's body fall off of my back. This was my chance! All I had to do was get back on my hands and knees. In the future, I would know what that position would mean in more than just a wrestling match. This war of flesh and blood would seem so small compared to the battle I would fight from within.

Laying side by side, I quickly untangled myself from the human pretzel we had contorted ourselves into. Once upright, I was able to lock my opponent in a head and arm. I had him on his back! Amidst all of the excitement, I heard a loud noise. It wasn't the crowd erupting in cheers as I was getting ready to secure my first win. It wasn't the referee's hand hitting the mat granting me the pin fall. It was the high-pitched whine of the buzzer, signaling the end of the period as well as the end of the match. There wasn't enough time left to score the pin. After all of that effort, I still lost, because my opponent had a higher score than I did.

Disappointed didn't even begin to describe how I felt at that moment in time. I glanced over at Coach Bennett, expecting to see the outward expression of how I felt on the inside. Instead, I saw a proud look in his eyes and a smile stretching from ear to ear. How could he be proud of me after I had come so close and yet still failed?

"This close," I gestured.

"This close," he returned the gesture.

I melted onto the gym floor as I struggled to catch my breath. Suddenly, the coach from the other team came over and wrapped his arm around me.

"Son," he whispered, "You've got more guts than any kid on my wrestling team. Great job!"

"Thank you," I said breathlessly.

I picked myself up off the floor and received warm embraces from several of my teammates.

Beyond the Mat

After I had worked so hard, wrestled my best, and come so close, I still lost. I again missed the mark. The very definition of sin means to "miss the mark." Often times, we try to work out our shortcomings on our own and we come "this close," yet still fail. Coach Bennett and my teammates showed me what God's love was like that day.

I was expecting Coach Bennett to scold me after I had come so close, but even after I wrestled my hardest and failed, they wrapped me up in a big hug and never let me go. In the same way, when we are serving God with everything we have and still fail, we expect God to scold us and hang His head in shame. In fact, just the opposite takes place. When we admit to Him we've done wrong and ask for His forgiveness, He picks us up, dusts us off and wraps us in a big hug.

The Streak Continues

If I am honest, the 2011-12 season was the most uneventful year of my career. It was a mirror image of my first year, except for me receiving a forfeit. I got to walk out onto the mat and have the referee raise my hand, only because the opposing team didn't have someone for me to wrestle in my weight class. That did not bring me any satisfaction whatsoever. If I was going to get my hand raised, it should be because I beat someone fair and square.

Other than that, every match I had, it was the same story. Step on the mat, get taken down, get beat. I had an amazing support system, but even still, I was getting visibly frustrated with myself. Everyone made it look so easy, executing moves so flawlessly, while it took every ounce of energy that I had just to keep from getting pinned.

I don't understand. I work harder than anybody else, yet I have nothing to show for it. Maybe I should just throw in the towel.

8

A Brave Chippewa

June 2012

A wise man will hear and increase in learning,
And a man of understanding will acquire wise counsel.

Proverbs 1:5 (NKJV)

Summer was in full swing and I was still feeling the sting of the previous wrestling season. I remained optimistic, though. I was going to be entering high school this upcoming year and thought that maybe the high school coaches would have some new tricks up their sleeves. The only problem was, how was I going to get stronger and improve my technique until then? Going to open mats once a week during the summer and doing regular push-ups and sit-ups helped some, but I knew I needed to do more if I wanted to succeed.

I was heavily engrossed in an epic wrestling match in Smackdown vs. Raw 2011 when my mom came bursting through the door.

"Your cousin, Joanna, just texted me. She wants to know if you want to go up to Michigan for a wrestling camp," Mom said.

"Yes!" I exclaimed.

My heart was bursting with excitement! This is precisely what I had been hoping for. I would be a fool to pass up such an amazing opportunity. I couldn't get registered quickly enough; the days couldn't pass fast enough. I wanted to be in Michigan now! I was confident that my skills would really improve being coached by a college wrestling coach.

The day finally arrived. With my bags in tow, I turned around and gave my parents a hug one last time. This was going to be the longest time I'd left home. I loaded my bags in my aunt's car and we were off. I have many fond memories with my Aunt Keitha and Uncle Jack. Almost every weekend when I was little, they would pick me up and we would go on an adventure. Whether it was going to see a movie, a game night, or even going on a hike, I was thrilled to add another experience to the long and growing list.

After four long hours, we finally arrived in a town known as Battle Creek, Michigan. The town sounded strangely familiar to me, and then it hit me- This was the town of legendary WWE superstar, Rob Van Dam.

I wonder if I'll get to meet him and get his autograph. It was a long shot, but a boy can dream, can't he?

We drove for another hour before reaching the town of Mt. Pleasant, where the college was located. After meeting up with my cousin, Joanna, we headed over to the campus. As we were driving over, my stomach twisted in knots, and my heart rate began to quicken. I began to wonder what kind of people I'd meet and how many friends

I would make. I was heading into completely new territory where I didn't know anybody.

As we arrived at the athletic complex for check-in, I spotted a sign which read: Central Michigan Chippewas. The University was named after the Chippewa Indian tribe, which was native to Michigan hundreds of years ago. In my mind, I began to note the similarities between Central Michigan University and my school, Logan Elm. The Logan Elm school district was named after an Indian chief named Logan. Chief Logan became famous for a speech that he gave under one of the largest elm trees ever recorded near the Circleville, Ohio area. The tree was 65 feet tall and 24 feet wide. Hence the name Logan Elm.

I walked inside the athletic complex and was met with a long line of people. In the meantime, I was in awe of the size of the facility. It had to have been the size of four or five Logan Elm athletic barns with a full-size indoor track looping the perimeter and at least a dozen wrestling mats covering the floor. The line finally shortened, and I got my check-in information. The dorm rooms were bare, with the basic necessities. My aunt and uncle left me to my own devices as I began to unpack. This was nerve-racking for a 14-year-old boy. The first session was later in the evening, so I thought it best to conserve my energy. As I was unpacking, a boy and his mom walked in.

Upon seeing me, he introduced himself. "Hi, I'm Luke," he said.

I shook his hand. "I'm Trevor."

Shortly afterward, another boy came in and introduced himself as Nate. We barely had time to get to know each other before it was time to go to the first session. All of the participants had to make the quarter mile trek together as a group. By the time we got to the athletic complex, I was already exhausted. I used most of my energy trying to keep up with everyone else, and I still had a two-hour wrestling practice to complete.

Despite my fatigue, I was still determined to finish the practice. We did a warm-up jog and agilities, just like I would at my school. The agilities were still a challenge, but I tried my very best. The coach called us over to the circle.

"Hi everybody. My name is Coach Borelli. I'm the head wrestling coach at CMU."

Coach Borelli instructed us to go through the shuffle and shot drill, just like we would back home at Logan Elm. We drilled many of the same basic moves that we would at my school. Being the impatient person I was, I wanted to learn the new moves right away. After the session, I began to make the long hike back. It wasn't long before everyone in the group started pulling ahead of me. Luckily, one of the camp counselors stayed behind me to keep me company.

"Your name is Trevor, right?" he asked.

"Yeah," I said.

"My name is Casey," he said.

"Nice to meet you," I replied.

Casey gave me a sympathetic look. "Do you want us to get you a ride to the athletic complex, so you don't have to walk so far next time?"

Everything in me wanted to say no. I guess you could call me stubborn. Throughout my life, people have always tried to do the smallest of tasks for me. While I appreciate the gesture, I always reaffirm I am capable of doing it myself.

"It's your stubbornness that got you out of the hospital, and it's your stubbornness that's going to put you back in the hospital," Mom would always say.

I knew it wasn't going to fly this time. If I was this tired after I've practiced and only walked the trail once, I could only imagine how tired I would be at the end of the week. Reluctantly, I said yes.

Once inside, I collapsed into a chair in the lobby and waited for opening night instructions. The counselors began to introduce themselves as the campers filed in. There was Alex, who looked to be carved out of marble, Casey and Josh, who both had similar physiques, and, last but not least, Robert. If I live to be 100, I will never forget "Rockin" Robert. His flamboyant tone and bubbly personality would light up any room. It's hard to put into words how unique of a character "Rockin" Robert was.

After the introductions, I joined the counselors and campers for dinner. I couldn't wait to test the rumors to see if college food was better than school food. It was fantastic! Meat loaf, fried potatoes, mac n' cheese, and pie. I was excited to go to college for the food alone! As we ate, I got to know Luke and Nate better. We talked about our favorite movies and what our future goals in wrestling were. When I confessed my goal was to win my first match, they were shocked.

"What? You've never won a match?" Luke asked.

"Nope," I responded.

He hesitated before speaking up again. "Do you mind if I ask what's wrong with your legs?"

I smiled and told him how I was born with cerebral palsy, and my doctors said I would never be able to walk or talk, yet here I was wrestling.

"That's awesome, dude… and you're ripped!" he exclaimed.

I managed a weak smile. "Thanks."

After dinner, most of the campers went outside to play ninja. I stayed in the lobby to mingle with the others and play a few rounds of 007 on the Nintendo 64 before retiring to my dorm for the night. My roommates soon joined me. We stayed up well past curfew, eating snacks and talking about life. I had only known them for a few short hours, but in those moments of solitude, I felt like I'd known them my whole life. I finally drifted off to sleep in the early hours of the morning. It's amazing how wrestlers just click. It truly is a brotherhood, no matter where you go.

9

A Brave Chippewa Part II

June 2012

Do all things without complaining and disputing, that you may become blameless and harmless, children of God without fault in the midst of a crooked and perverse generation, among whom you shine as lights in the world.

Philippians 2:14-15 (NKJV)

Day 2

Coming out of a deep sleep, I silenced my alarm clock and placed my feet on the cold tile floor. As I tried to stand up, intense pain shot through my feet. I tried to stand a second time. This time, I used the head of the bed to push myself up. With every step I took, pain radiated from my feet to my lower back. It was a sign that I had overdone it the night before. With my roommates still asleep, I quietly made my way over to the showers to get ready for the day. I have to wake up earlier than most, because it takes me twenty to thirty minutes to shower safely.

I couldn't wait to see what the day had in store. As I walked into the lobby, Alex was there, waiting for me.

"Are you ready for your ride to breakfast?" he asked. I looked and sitting outside the door was a Gator. Coming from a family who eats, sleeps, and breathes Farmall red, I was never so happy to see one of those green machines in my life. It would help me conserve much needed energy.

After breakfast, it was time for the first session of the day. I walked into the athletic complex and noticed two huge men in the center mat. Coach Borelli introduced them as Zach and CJ. They were wrestlers at CMU, and they were going to help coach. My confidence began to build as I was able to execute most of the moves they were demonstrating. As we were working on our next takedown, I looked up just in time to see someone on the other side of the room vomit into one of the strategically placed trash cans at the corner of the mat. They looked to be doing several different cardio exercises and the coach was yelling at the kids like a drill sergeant.

"What are they doing?" I asked.

"That's the intensity wrestling camp," my partner said. I gave him a puzzled look. "They have to get up at 5 in the morning to run a mile," he continued. A part of me wanted to try it out of curiosity, but I quickly realized I may have been pushing my luck. My rule of thumb is always, if you see me running, you'd better be running too, because something is chasing me!

At the end of the session, Coach Borelli called us into a circle. "You guys have been doing great so far," he encouraged. "Tomorrow evening, we are going to be hosting a tournament to test your skills. Be sure to treat your body right, so you can perform at your best."

Sweet, I'll be able to see how much I've improved!

We were dismissed, and after a quick lunch, it was time for the afternoon session. I was more excited than usual about this session because Zach announced that we were going to be working on referees' (top and bottom) position. The first top technique we worked on was riding legs. Zach started out in normal referees' position with his arm around the belly and his other hand cupped around the elbow. He then looped his right leg in between CJ's legs and wrapped it around CJ's right leg. He repeated the process on the left side and thus, CJ was immobilized.

"You have control of your opponent's lower body," Zach said. "You can pretty much do whatever you want with him."

I could see where this technique might be a problem for me, but I am never one to make decisions on my physical ability based on assumption alone. I got with my partner and I started to lift my leg when I felt a familiar pain in my hip. Every time I would try to wrap my leg around my partner's, my hip would begin to dislocate. I simply was not flexible enough to do the drill. I did push-ups while my partner found someone else to drill with. I was a little disappointed to find out that most of the things that we did on top during the session had to do with riding legs. Even still, I always tried to find ways to modify the move.

The next series of moves focused on the bottom position. Zach demonstrated a new version of the stand-up that looked to be easier for me to perform.

"When the ref blows the whistle, you're going to slide your knees forward and put all of your power in the side that he doesn't have ahold of," Zach said. "Once you're up, break the guy's grip by using your hip to create a gap and then put your thumbs in the gap to get free."

We broke off, and I was the first to try it. I slid my legs forward just as instructed, and I tried to push up on my right leg. While this variation did make things a little easier, I still had to focus a great deal on keeping my balance. Once on my feet, I was able to break my partner's grip and get free. Another challenge presented itself when my partner attempted the move. Whenever he would stand up, he would do it so fast I was not able to keep up, and I would fall. I was able to adapt by keeping ahold of his waist and using his body to hoist myself up.

I left the afternoon session with my confidence continuing to grow. I may have had trouble riding legs, but you don't need to ride legs to win a match. The things I had learned beforehand were so invaluable that the issue of riding legs almost didn't matter. I was certain that I was going to win a match in the upcoming season. Despite my circumstances, I am a competitive person. If I won a match during the tournament, I wouldn't be as excited as I would if I won a match during the active season.

After dinner and relaxation time, it was time for the evening session. It was a live drill session, which means each drill is meant to reflect a wrestling match, except you don't go for the pin. I fared well and got many compliments on my strength and determination from the people I drilled with. It felt good to know that I was having such a positive impact on my peers.

Later that night a group of guys and I wanted to take a trip to the 7-11 a few blocks away. The receptionist gave me a sympathetic look and said, "We aren't able to get you a ride this late at night."

"I'll walk," I said.

"Are you sure?" he asked, surprised. "It's almost a quarter of a mile hike one way."

I assured him that I was positive and rushed to join the rest of the group. It wasn't long, though, before my fatigue throughout the day began to catch up with me, and I began to fall behind from the rest of the group. One of the camp counselors that accompanied us noticed that I was falling behind and fell back to join me.

For someone with cerebral palsy, any surface that isn't flat can be very difficult to walk on. After dodging many cracks in the sidewalk and carefully crossing over some hilly, uneven terrain, we finally made it to our destination. All of that work was totally worth the Coca–Cola and Mountain Dew slushy (mixed together) and a family–size bag of Cool Ranch Doritos. On the way back, the fatigue really started to set in.

"Come on, you can do it. We're almost there," Casey said.

Once inside my dorm room, I collapsed onto my bed as Nate, Luke, and Joey welcomed me. We stayed up well past curfew talking about life and our dreams. It's amazing how you can grow so close to a group of people in such a short amount of time.

Day Three

I woke up the next day full of adrenaline. Today was tournament day and I was finally going to see how much progress I truly made. I wolfed down my breakfast and made my way to the morning session. Zach introduced a new drill in which someone leaned back into their partner with only their head and neck supported. The person who was offering the support had to let go, allowing the other person to free fall. The person falling then had to swivel his hips and twist his body to avoid falling flat on his back. This was to help our timing with the sprawl in order to avoid getting taken down.

I had no problem supporting my partner's neck and letting him fall; my problem came when it was my turn to sprawl. I would find myself falling but unable to react fast enough. I knew what I needed to do, but my body wouldn't allow me. I always ended up falling flat on my back. Both the morning and afternoon session consisted of light drilling and live wrestling to prepare us for the upcoming tournament.

Time seemed to fly and as the sun began to set, the tournament was set to begin. I was eager to see how much I had grown. I could tell that I had grown not only as a wrestler throughout my time at camp, but as a person, too.

"It will be a double elimination style tournament," Coach Borelli said, "You lose twice, you're done. However, we will have exhibition matches and you can challenge anyone you want after you're done."

My first match came up in no time at all and I was standing face to face with a tall, skinny-as-a-rail opponent. As soon as the whistle sounded, I dove for the leg and held on for dear life. I knew I needed to get behind him in order to get the takedown, but it was as if my body was frozen. I couldn't move. It was as if all I could focus on was keeping ahold of his leg and not letting go.

The clock ran out and we went into second period. My opponent selected top and I got down on my hands and knees. The whistle blew, and I slid my legs forward to try to desperately apply what I had learned. As I brought my right leg up, my opponent quickly switched to the opposite side to lock me in a cradle. I was able to break the grip to avoid the pin, but just as quickly, he rolled me on my back with the half nelson and got the victory.

The loss stung but I didn't lose hope. I still had another match. Not even twenty minutes after my first match, it was time for my second. I walked out onto the mat to meet an opponent who was built almost like me. Immediately after the match started, I dove for the leg. This move proved to be fatal, because as soon as I tried to get up on my knees, he broke free and rolled me over by using the half nelson. As I fought to get free, my opponent immobilized my legs to keep me from fighting off my back, Ultimately, he won the match.

I walked off the mat, disappointed. It seemed like I didn't make any progress at all. I knew that it was because of the offensive approach I was taking, but I how was I going to fix it? Holding onto somebody's leg doesn't win a match. I was over looking at the brackets posted on the wall when I heard a voice call from behind me. Standing behind me was a boy a little bit shorter than me with brown hair.

"Do you want to wrestle?" he asked.

I was taken aback by this sudden challenge having wrestled only five minutes before, but I gladly accepted. Once the referee was in place, we began. The kid shot in for a leg. As I sprawled against him, he crumbled under my weight. I got 2 points for a takedown and rolled him over with the half nelson. After getting the 5 count, the ref slapped the mat. I had won the match in 30 seconds. While I was happy I won, it didn't feel momentous because it wasn't during the actual season. Furthermore, I couldn't shake the feeling that something wasn't right. He felt much lighter than most 126 pounders

"How much do you weigh?" I asked.

"90 pounds," he said.

My suspicions were correct. That's why I was able to beat him so easily. I thanked him for a good match and went on to watch my roommates compete. Luke placed 2nd while Nate and Joey were eliminated a little later. After the tournament we went back to our room and enjoyed one another's company. Since it was our last night together, we reflected on what we learned individually and promised to stay in touch with each other.

Day Four

I finished packing my things for the trip home and joined the team in the athletic building for pizza. Coach Borelli stopped me as I was heading back to my dorm to get my stuff.

"You did a great job this week," he said, "I'm proud of you."

I said my goodbyes to the coaches and my fellow campers and headed back to Ohio. One very important thing that I learned in my time at Central Michigan University was that, no matter where you go in the world, wrestling is a universal brotherhood. We have different bloodlines and backgrounds, yet we all bleed the same blood, sweat the same sweat and cry the same tears. There is not a brotherhood that is tighter knit than that of the wrestling community.

As I was heading home, I was scrolling through social media. I came to one post that stopped me in my tracks. My mom had shared an email from the camp coordinator that Joanna had shared with her. It reads:

"Hi, Joanna, just wanted to let you know how "outstanding" we all think Trevor is. We have had the opportunity to meet him when picking him up to take him to and from dorm/camp, etc. How inspiring to see a young man who has the will and desire to do all this and doesn't complain. He is an example of what we all should be. Pass that along, would you, to your parents and to Trevor's parents as well. They should be proud and know we are the ones blessed and honored in having him here!"

I may have moments of discouragement after tasting defeat so many times but notes like this remind me why I fell in love with wrestling in the first place. They motivate me to keep trying. I was going to win my first match even if it took the rest of my career.

Freshman Year (9th Grade)

10

Entering the Big Leagues

November 2012

And when the Philistine looked about and saw David, he disdained him; for he was only a youth, ruddy and good-looking.

1 Samuel 17:42 (NKJV)

My heart was pounding as I made my way to the wrestling barn for the first day of wrestling practice. I was so excited to finally be wrestling at the high school level. We have more meets, the season is longer, and I was going to be reunited with teammates from my first year who I had grown to love. I was also going to be under the coaching of the infamous Logan Elm duo, Coach Barnes and Coach Polly. It couldn't get any better!

I was overjoyed to see everyone. Dustin Miller, Thomas, DJ, Dominick, Justin Payne and many more all made a return. We had some new faces as well. Practice started, and we did our normal routine of a warm-up jog and our agilities. I could definitely tell I was stronger than last year, but I still couldn't do a majority of the agilities without losing my balance. Everyone understood by now, so it didn't bother me as much.

For our first day of practice, Coach Polly and Coach Barnes went over the basics. My drilling partner for the day was Justin. I went first and shot in for a double leg takedown. I lifted Justin into the air and returned him to the mat with a thud.

"You've gotten a lot stronger," he said.

We drilled a little while longer and then slowly transitioned into live wrestling. One thing I loved about my team, they never took it easy on me just because I have cerebral palsy. My teammates beat me up during practice, just like they would anyone else. It was the most fun I ever had getting my butt kicked. Through it all, they kept encouraging me to do better and never give up.

At this point, practice was almost over, and we were all getting tired. Coach Polly called us over to the edge of the mat and split us all up into two groups.

"I want you to sprint down and back until I say stop," Coach Polly said, "One group goes and then the other."

I took off and immediately fell behind the others. That didn't bother me, though, because I knew I was going as fast as I could. We did these five times before we were told to stop, and, just like that, two hours flew by. As we gathered in a huddle, Coach Barnes congratulated us on a job well done.

"In a couple weeks, we're going to have alpha weigh-ins," Coach Barnes said. "They're going to check your hydration, your body fat percentage, and your weight. Be smart if you want to drop," he encouraged.

"By the way," Coach Polly said, "Wednesday's practice is going to suck."

I walked away curious, yet terrified as to what he meant. I stepped on the scale, and after a few seconds, it read 126 lbs. It was safe to say I didn't need to cut weight. I was already stronger than most people in my weight class; it was just a matter of getting my body to do what I wanted it to do. Though it was going to be a challenge wrestling kids four years older than me, I was excited to see what this new chapter of my career was going to bring.

Wear 'em out Wednesday

I walked into practice with a group of guys, and as we walked in, Coach Polly had a mile-wide grin on his face. He warned us a couple days prior that Wednesday's practice was going to suck, and now we were even more scared.

"So, what's this practice going to be like?" DJ asked.

"Oh, you'll love it," Coach Polly said, sarcastically.

Everything started like normal, until Coach Polly instructed us to grab a weight off the weight rack.

"Halos," he instructed. I lifted the 25-lb. weight above my head and began to move it in a circular motion. After about 10 seconds, Coach Polly yelled out the next exercise.

"Steering wheels." We had to hold the weight out in front of us and turn it as if we were driving a car. I looked over and saw Coach Polly looked to be setting up some kind of boot-camp-style obstacle course.

"Diamond push-ups," he barked as he continued to work. We set our plates on the ground, formed a diamond with our hands around the center of the plate, and did push-ups.

"Mason-twists," Coach Polly yelled out. We sat down and had to bring the weight from one side of the body to the other. At this point, every inch of my body felt like it was on fire. We performed this circuit three times before we had to stop.

After the circuit, Coach Polly split us up into three-man teams. He instructed me to do push-ups and sit-ups off to the side because this required a lot of balance.

"Three of you at a time are going to carry a wrestling mat around the room," Coach Polly began. He pointed to a bench sitting on the mat, "You have to find a way around this bench. You cannot simply walk around it. You have to be creative and work as a team."

I could see why Coach Polly cautioned me about this exercise. I wouldn't have the balance nor the speed to keep up with everyone else. While I have never let my limitations define me, I had to be realistic about them as well. I didn't want to get hurt and not be able to wrestle. I admit, I watched with glee as DJ, Johnny, and Thomas marched around the room with a 100+ pound mat on their backs. They stopped in their tracks when they got to the bench.

I watched in amazement, as one by one, each of them stepped over the bench as they were holding onto the mat. When each of the teams finished the course, we jumped straight into live wrestling. We did five rounds of live wrestling and went straight into another round of cardio. Coach Polly gave us a list of exercises, and we had to count down from 10. We had to do 10 mountain climbers, 10 jumping jacks, 10 single leg lunges, 10 push-ups, and 10 grass drills. Then 9. Then 8 and so on.

From there, we did another five rounds of live wrestling. Everyone was running on fumes at this point. Trying to grapple DJ was next to impossible with his body greased with sweat. This is what separates wrestling from any other sport in the world. You can't take a break on the sidelines or substitute a player, just because you're tired. There is no one else to fall back on. It's all you.

In life, just like in wrestling, there is no one else to fall back on. It's all you. You are responsible for your own decisions and actions. You can't blame someone else when you make a mistake. Accept it, learn from it, and move on.

Coach Polly blew his whistle and told us to line up on the edge of that mat, as he began to set cones down.

"Run to every cone and then run back," he said. "Three suicides, and you're done."

I blasted off for every cone as fast as my legs would carry me. Again, I fell behind the rest of the group, but I knew I was trying my hardest, and I still got the job done. After we completed the suicides, we all gathered in a huddle.

"Great job today, guys," Coach Polly said. "Just so you know, it's going to be like this every Wednesday."

Coach Polly dubbed these intense weekly practices "Wear 'em out Wednesdays." Due to my increased use of energy, it took everything I had and more to complete these practices. You might have a day or even a week that completely wears you out, but Jesus says, "Come all who are weary, and I will give you rest." When we rely on Jesus as our strength, we will never wear out.

The Alpha Male- 11/17/12

The following Saturday, I heeded the coach's advice and attempted to stay hydrated throughout the day. I drank throughout the early morning and continued to drink on the way over to the wrestling barn. As I was getting ready, I estimated that I probably drank close to a half- gallon of water and Gatorade or more in two hours. Unfortunately, I soon began to regret my decision. The hydration test wasn't for another half-hour, and they call each weight class at random.

I was in agony as I waited for my weight class to be called. As luck would have, my weight class was the last one to be called. Not only that, I was also the last person in line, and the line to the bathroom was at least 70 people deep.

"Next time, you won't drink so much, huh?" Micah said with a smirk.

I made it through the ordeal without any incidents, but I definitely learned my lesson. Stay hydrated throughout the week and don't drink everything at one time, or else "urine trouble" (pun intended).

First Meet- Circleville Kiwanis- 12/1/12

There's something about the first meet of the season that's special. You have to start getting used to getting up early again, stay disciplined on your weight, and there is a feeling of nervousness as you go to have your first match of the season. It doesn't matter how experienced you are, you just can't shake it. You have goals that you want to accomplish, but you aren't sure of what triumphs or hardships the season may bring. For me, I still had one goal–to win a match.

Nothing rivals the feeling of warming up as a team and looking around at your competition. You can feel the anticipation building as you jog around the mat, wondering which one of them you're up against. Nothing beats the warm feeling you get when you look up into the stands and see your parents, family, and friends who have come to cheer you on. Nothing beats the sense of camaraderie that covers you as you go to war with and cheer on your brothers on the mat. Nothing comes close to the intensity of a hard-fought match. Fans, coaches, and teammates alike, all standing on their feet, shouting at the top of their lungs, hoping that their son, their teammate will come out on top. All of this and more embodies the sport of wrestling. It's something that never gets old.

High school wrestling is a little different than middle school wrestling. While the rules pretty much stay the same, the season and the periods are longer. Instead of 1:30 per period, it's now 2:00 per period. Plus, this is the time when colleges start to scout, and, as a freshman, I was possibly going to be wrestling people four years older than me! I was more than up for the challenge. I look at every match as an opportunity to win, no matter who they are. After all, nobody expects the underdog to win.

Before I knew it, my weight class was called, and I went over to prepare for my match. This was going to be my first varsity wrestling match, so I was determined to make it a win. My name was called, and I made my way over to the head table. I was going to be wrestling someone named Troy, from Circleville. Troy was a little bit taller than me and stocky. Circleville and Logan Elm are huge rivals, so I was bound and determined to beat him. We assumed our positions, and the match started. I dropped to my knees and grabbed ahold of his leg. In an instant, he was able to break free, but I was actually able to roll away from him to avoid getting taken down.

I was definitely quicker and more limber than last year. I could hear Coach Barnes shouting commands, but it was all a blur. I rose to my feet and circled Troy for a few seconds, before being taken down and locked in a cradle. I got pinned in 1:05, but I wasn't disappointed. I performed well in that match, and I still had an entire season to go.

I shook Troy's hand, and I went over to shake Coach Brad's and Kevin's hands. As I shook Kevin's hand, he leaned into me and said, "You're our favorite."

After spending some time cheering on my teammates, my second match came in the blink of an eye. I ran out on the mat, ready for war, only to get taken down and pinned in thirty seconds. It was a moment of disappointment, for sure, but I still had one more match left for the day. I was going to be sure to make that one count.

My third match of the day came, and I was going up against a wiry kid in a black and blue singlet. As soon as the match started, I was taken down instantly. Shaken but not beaten, I was not going to let the same thing as last time happen to me in this match. I bore down onto the mat and became immovable. My opponent tried to roll me onto my back for a whole period, but he couldn't do it. At the end of the first period, I heard his coach cry out;

"Come on, this kid isn't going to quit!"

I anticipated a much more aggressive offense. I was on bottom in the referee's position, and he was on top. He picked up my foot and drove me to the ground, forcing me to eat a face full of mat. He locked in the half-nelson, but he was not going to put me on my back if I had anything to say about it. We went through another period of an utter stalemate, as no one was able to get the advantage over the other. We entered the third period and we were both exhausted. I hadn't let my opponent have any opportunities to pin me. If he was going to win, it was going to be by points.

I was on top this time. I dragged my tired body and got into position. My opponent was able to move quickly enough for him to regain control. All of a sudden, he was on top of me and cradled me so tightly, my knees touched my forehead. I was stuck, there was nothing I could do. He won by pin fall in the middle of the third period. I walked off the mat and shook the opposing coach's hand.

"Outstanding effort," he said. I smiled back at him. I couldn't be disappointed after a match like that.

I sat on the bench next to DJ as he was cheering on Dustin White. His match was at the tail end of the third period, and it was tied 5-5.

"Come on, Dusty, you got to go!" DJ screamed.

Other teammates were around, watching the spectacle, and fans were on their feet, screaming in anticipation. With five seconds left, Dustin hit a double leg to secure the victory and make the score 7-5. People in the stands shouted with glee and moaned with disappointment.

"Atta boy, Dusty," DJ yelled.

Atta boy. That is what DJ told every one of our teammates every time they won a match. I so very desperately wanted DJ to say, "Atta boy" to me.

11

The Underdog Strikes

December 8, 2012

And let endurance have its perfect result, so that you may be perfect and complete, lacking in nothing.

James 1:4 (NASB)

If you were to add up every match that I've had from my 7th grade year up until this point, including pre- and post-season matches, the total would be 71 matches. That means I have lost 71 times in a row. At this point, I was getting very discouraged and frustrated. It seemed like no matter how hard I tried, no matter how long I stayed after practice to practice some more, and no matter how much time I spent working out, I never saw the fruits of my training.

Our next meet was at Logan High school and I was already warned ahead of time that the 126 lb. weight class in this tournament was going to be tough. Still, I got up the morning of the tournament ready for a fight! I didn't care how tough any of my opponents were, they were in for the fight of their lives! I made weight with a few pounds to spare. The great thing about cerebral palsy and using three to five times more energy than the average person, is you have an extremely fast metabolism. Everything I ate, I burned off just as quickly. I became the envy of the entire team.

As I prepared for each match, I wondered if this is going to be the one where I finally won. I rehearsed all of the moves I had honed from the week's practice during warm-ups and vowed to do my best. My first match of the day came against a kid from Logan. The referee blew the whistle, and we went to battle. After a few seconds, I was taken down to the mat. I continue to fight as he attempted to roll me over. After a brief struggle, he managed to roll me over on my back and pinned me in one minute flat. A wave of disappointment came over me as I once again lay flat on my back as my opponent stood over me in victory. Seventy-two losses.

I slumped back into the bleachers and looked on as my teammates competed. They make it look so easy, and winning a match wasn't that uncommon for them. My next match came, and I swore to myself that I was going to last at least three periods. I was more determined than ever. I locked up with my opponent with more force than ever before. He countered my intensity with a double leg take down straight to my back. He locked my arms and legs in place, and the ref hit the mat for the pin fall. I got pinned in fifteen seconds. Seventy-three losses.

My anger and frustration had reached a boiling point. I hit the mat out of frustration and stormed over to Coach Barnes. He gave me a stern look and pulled me off to the side.

"Don't hit the mat again," he said. "I know you're frustrated, but realize that nobody in this gym works harder than you do. You're an inspiration to your teammates and everyone in here. Don't give up."

He sent me on my way to let his words resonate. I ran into Thomas in the cafeteria, and he must've sensed my glum mood.

"What's wrong, Trev?" he asked

"You guys can win a match and make it look so easy," I said. "I try so hard and can't even win one."

He studied me for a moment before speaking up. "Yeah, but you've got something most of us don't."

"What's that?" I asked.

"Heart," he said. I managed a smile. Maybe I was having more of an impact on people than I thought

During the break, the team got in its traditional huddle and hung out before the next round started. We were gossiping, laughing, and having a good time when I looked up and saw that my dad had a smile on his face.

"What?" I asked out of curiosity.

"You have to wrestle a girl next round," he said.

This is either going to be really interesting or really awkward. If I lost to a girl, my teammates would never let me live it down.

The time came when the third round began, and I had to wrestle a girl from Trimble High School. I was trembling in my boots, even before the match started. We positioned ourselves on the mat, and the referee blew the whistle. The girl lunged at me and fell flat. I saw the opportunity, locked in the half, and rolled her on her back. Out of the corner of my eye, I saw Justin's eyes get as big as dinner plates, and an entire gym leap to their feet as the ref counted to five. Even the Trimble wrestling team was cheering for me! The girl was able to roll back onto her belly.

"Do it again!" Coach Barnes yelled.

I did as he said and was able to put her on her back yet again, but this time only for a one count. The noise in the room was deafening. I could barely hear myself think. She was able to bring herself up to her hands and knees, and I lost my own base. The tables were turned. She was on top, and I was on bottom, and she managed to roll me onto my back for a five count. She got two points for a reversal and three points for a near pin fall.

Going into the second period, it was tied 5-5. I had the option to choose, and I chose top. As soon as the ref blew the whistle, I hit a cross face, and she folded onto the mat. I was able to roll her up for another near fall, making it 8-5. I tried again and again to pin her, but she was persistent. She was not going down without a fight, and I would expect nothing less. We were both growing tired, and the second period was nearing its end.

The buzzer chimed for the end of the second period, and she opted to choose bottom. She was going to try and get some last second desperation points. If I can just hold the lead, I'll win! The whistle blew, and I grabbed ahold of her leg and drove her into the mat. She started to get back up on her base, but I stopped her by grabbing her wrists. I was so close, I was not going to lose! I locked in the half nelson once more, but she wouldn't budge. I had to quickly get back into position and wait for the clock to run out. Only ten seconds left! 5.. 4.. 3.. 2.. 1..

The buzzer sounded. I actually won the match! The final score was 8-5. Cheers erupted from the stands as I got my hand raised in victory for the very first time. I was finally the one who was able to circle the win column on the bout sheet. The smile on my dad's face said it all.

"That was one of the highlights of my career," Coach Barnes said. "Watching Trevor Lane win a match."

I looked over at the section of bleachers where my teammates were sitting and noticed it was empty. I walked into the hallway, and there they all were to meet me in the middle.

"You did it, man!" Thomas said as he and Dustin both embraced me with a hug.

Justin, with a look of pride in his eyes, hugged me as well. I got high-fives and handshakes from the others. This was a moment that I didn't want to end. I spotted DJ running toward me with a smile a mile wide. He picked me up in a sweaty embrace, having just wrestled a match while I was wrestling.

"Atta boy," DJ proclaimed.

That night I posted on social media the following:

"Sometimes, at night, I would have dreams about winning my first match. But I don't have to do that anymore, because I just made it a reality. Big thanks to all of my teammates and coaches."

The love and support I received was nothing short of amazing. All the hard work I put in finally paid off. It took me three years and seventy-four matches, but I finally won a match. A victory wasn't the only thing I obtained, I also had new-found courage to continue wrestling.

Beyond the Mat

You might be like me. You might be fighting the battle of your life and are about ready to give up. You've been fighting for years, and you just can't take it anymore. Don't give up. In my moments of deep discouragement, my teammates and coaches picked me back up and pushed me forward. It took me six years to walk on my own and three years to win my first match. Keep fighting. Whether it's walking independently or achieving some other long-term goal, don't give up! It might take days, weeks, months, or even years, but you will get there.

Sometime later, I received a text from a friend of mine who I hadn't connected with for some time. He said he had an addiction to pills and would take them regularly to get high. However, after he heard I won my first match despite all of my challenges, he threw his pills away and vowed to never use them again. It was a humbling experience that I will never forget. He is still clean 8 years later.

12

Setbacks

January 2013

And not only this, but we also exult in our tribulations, knowing that tribulation brings about perseverance; and perseverance, proven character; and proven character, hope; and hope does not disappoint, because the love of God has been poured out within our hearts through the Holy Spirit who was given to us.

Romans 5:3-5 (NASB)

It was the beginning of the new year, and one of the most anticipated wrestling meets of the season was on the horizon. The Logan Elm Dual Invitational. I had watched snippets of the meet over the past couple of years, and it looked unique. It was a tournament, but you wrestled each team one at a time, which is one of the reasons why I looked forward to competing in it. Everyone was close together and watched each other's match.

My excitement was building. The tournament was only days away, and there was still nobody to challenge me for the varsity spot. I was getting ready for practice when Dominick walked into the locker room.

"You and I have to wrestle off," Dominick said.

I gave him a puzzled look. "What do you mean?"

"I want to wrestle up a weight class because there is a kid I want to wrestle at 126," he said.

My heart dropped into my stomach. I knew Dominick was better than me, but I wasn't about to just hand him the varsity spot. As everyone gathered around to watch, Dominick and I took our positions. We locked up, and Dominick instantly blasted me with a double leg takedown. I rolled onto my belly and prepared for Dominick's assault. He knew me well. He closed any gap I could pry at to escape the half nelson. I was nearly defenseless.

I fought him off as long as I could with mere core strength alone, but eventually, he pinned me a little over a minute into the first period. I was not going to be wrestling in the Logan Elm Invitational this year. Disappointment quickly took over as there would be no room for extra wrestlers in the tournament. It was the first time I had ever been angry about not being able to wrestle.

Beyond the Mat

Disappointment and anger are inevitable in life. The question is, what are you going to do about it? Are you going to sit and let it fester and feel sorry for yourself, or are you going to use it as motivation to better yourself?

If You Give a Wrestler Duct Tape

If it's one thing wrestlers know how to do, it's pulling a prank. Coach Barnes was the technology teacher at the junior high, so we were assigned to wait in his room until weigh-ins. I was still feeling the sting of my loss to Dominick and really didn't want to talk to anyone. This was the tournament I had looked forward to wrestling in the most, and I wasn't even going to get to wrestle as JV.

Our 170–pounder, Joey was asleep in one of the chairs while the rest of us mingled. Suddenly, DJ got a mischievous smile on his face. DJ picked up the duct tape from the corner of Coach Barnes' desk and began to wrap the tape around Joey's legs and the legs of the chair. DJ set the chair on the floor with Joey in it. At this point, Joey woke up to see both of his legs wrapped in duct tape. As a finishing touch, DJ wrapped a strip of duct tape around Joey's head.

"I can't move," Joey said, as the rest of us howled in laughter. Joey sighed in relief as DJ began to free him from his sticky situation. Cameras were rolling as this ordeal was taking place, and I was sure this was going to be a viral sensation. Joey's legs were free, but his troubles were far from over. We still had to remove the tape on his head. DJ grabbed the end of the tape and yanked. Joey screamed as hair was stripped from his head. We all doubled over in laughter as Joey stood up with a bright red mark on his forehead. Joey was not angry, and he didn't get seriously hurt. In fact, he laughed right along with us. We were just doing what brothers do.

As the tournament drew closer, I headed out with the team to warm up. During that time, the fact that I wasn't wrestling in the tournament burned inside of me. I was determined to never let that happen again. This wasn't the final destination, only a setback. I was eager, though, to see how everyone would fare.

The Aftermath

"Seventh place at our own tournament!" Coach Barnes yelled. "Are you satisfied with seventh place?"

We all nodded in shameful disapproval. What transpired next was one of the hardest practices to date. Insane amounts of cardio and live drilling with no sign of stopping. By the end, we could barely stand.

"I hope you've learned a new respect for this sport," Coach Barnes said. "If you don't have respect for this sport, get out of this room!" He pointed his finger at me, "If you don't have respect for what that man does every time he steps on the mat, get out. I expect a better performance this week."

Another Close Call

That next Saturday morning, with the fear of God instilled in us, we vowed to do better than 7th place at Grandview Heights. It was a double-elimination tournament, so I knew I had to perform at my best. My first match was nothing to write home about. My first opponent was the guy who was projected to win the whole tournament. I lost in 45 seconds, but I gave it my all. I wasn't too hard on myself. The momentum I carried from winning my first match gave me the confidence that I could do it again if I just kept trying.

During my second match, I wrestled a kid named John. He looked nervous as we lined up to start the match. We locked up, and he was able to take me down with ease. I fought him off until the end of the second period. The score was 2-0 going into the second period. I was chosen to start on top. Once the match restarted, I nailed him with a cross face. He fell to the ground, but instantly got up on all fours and turned to face me. I wrapped my arms around him and took him to his back. No sooner did the referee begin the count, John rolled over onto his belly. I had no control over him, so he was able to break free to get an escape point. John took me down again to take us into the third period.

I had to go on bottom this time, but I was actually able to perform a stand up and get the escape point. Once on my feet, I pushed John outside of the circle, causing us to go out of bounds. We had to restart in our previous position. The ref blew the whistle, and I was knocked onto my stomach. He desperately tried to roll me over, but I was able to get back on my hands and knees to sit out. John wrapped his arms around my waist, and I pushed back against him to try and turn into him and escape. People were on their feet and I could hear Coach Barnes yelling, but couldn't make out what he was saying.

The referee called a stalemate because neither one of us was getting the advantage over the other. We got back into referee's position, and John picked my right leg up and drove me into the mat. In a last-ditch effort, he locked in that half nelson as tightly as he could and flipped me onto my back. I fought back with everything that I had left, but my body was too tired. I got pinned toward the end of the third period.

I walked off the mat with a smile on my face. I couldn't be disappointed in a match like that. I gave it my all and could tell John did, too.

"Great match, champ." Coach Barnes said. "Now it's time to get ready for the real wrestling season."

13

Winning Isn't Everything

February 2013

Let your light so shine before men, that they may see your good works and glorify your Father in heaven.

Matthew 5:16 (NKJV)

It's true what they say, time flies when you're having fun. The few months of the regular season seemed like a few weeks. Before I knew it, it was time for the post-season festivities. The post-season in high school is divided up into three sections: Sectionals, Districts and State. Each level of competition takes place between February and March and is designed to separate the men from the boys. Only the best of the best makes it to the State level. Every varsity wrestler gets to wrestle at sectionals, but you must place in the top four in your weight class to advance to Districts. Once you make it to Districts, you must place in the top four in your weight class to go to State.

Fortunately for me, Dominick dropped back down to 120 lbs. leaving the 126 lb. weight class open. Coach Polly warned me that the 126 lb. class was one of the hardest ones to make it to state, but I welcomed the challenge, I was just excited to have the opportunity to possibly wrestle at such a high level. This wasn't going to be like middle school, where you could pay to go to State if you wanted to. This was going to be a war. This is when the real season begins.

Sectionals Day 1

My mind was racing as I prepared for my first match of the night. My first match was going to be against the number one seed; the person who was projected to win the whole tournament. Even though the odds were stacked against me, I was not going to back down. I walked onto the mat with the mindset that I was going to go to State. I stepped on the line, the referee blew the whistle, and we were off. I was taken down seconds after the match started and put into a pin combination. After forty seconds, the referee slapped the mat for the pin fall.

After my first match, Coach Barnes informed me I had a bye the next round.

"Looks like you won't wrestle again until tomorrow," Coach Barnes said, "And you won't know who you'll wrestle until then either."

Sectionals Day 2- Knul and Void

I woke up the next morning with resounding determination. Today was going to be my last chance to even get close to making it to Districts. I didn't know who I was going to wrestle, but I was going to make sure they never wanted to wrestle me again. I had a new-found intensity and I wanted to prove to everyone that I could wrestle with the best of them despite my disability. Even though I had won a match, I was still the underdog because nobody expected me to win.

As the time drew near for the tournament to begin, Coach Barnes revealed who each of us was going to be wrestling. I was going to be wrestling a kid named Tyler Knul from Circleville. He had an impressive record and nearly won his match from the day before. I had another fight on my hands, and that was okay.

Coach Barnes looked at me and smiled, "Go get 'em, champ."

My name was called, and I walked over to the head table with nervous anticipation. Tyler had that pretty boy look, but I knew not to judge a book by its cover. We took our positions, and the referee blew the whistle. In a split second, I was flat on my back. Tyler quickly switched positions and locked me in a cradle. I kicked and fought with all my might, but it was not enough. The match was over in 15 seconds.

I couldn't hide my disappointment. I shook hands with Tyler and his coach. My freshman season was over and was not how I wanted it to end.

"You had a good season, champ," Coach Barnes encouraged.

I got dressed and walked over to the middle of the court with Coach Barnes. I watched as Dominick, DJ, Johnny, Micah, and Isaiah all made their way to Districts and I didn't. The competitor in me was relentless. It killed me inside and made me want to work even harder.

"Hey, Coach, do you think I'll win another match" I asked.

"I'm sure you will." He paused for a moment before continuing. "But I wouldn't beat yourself up over it if you don't. You're an inspiration to your team and everyone who knows you. You've got more guts than anybody I know."

I smiled as I continued to watch the heavyweight championship match. Out of the corner of my eye, I saw Thomas coming and he handed me a plain white envelope.

"Hey, Trev," he said. "Some random lady wanted me to give this to you."

I carefully opened up the letter and was shocked at what it said:

Dear Trevor,

Watching you yesterday and today has been so uplifting and inspiring. I know the effort, hard work, commitment, guts, and more hard work wrestling requires. I don't know your challenges, but from where I sit, you have overcome most of those before you step out on that mat. I have cried for your disappointment and heartbreak, praised your dedication and winning spirit. Don't for one instant think you have not won. You won it all even before entering the ring. I don't need to see them raise your arm to know you have won—you are a superior champion!! Wishing you much success in all you do- you have the drive and spirit to do anything.

With much admiration,

A granduverous fan!

The timing of the letter was uncanny. It was exactly what I needed to hear. It was in that moment I realized that I didn't need to win a match to prove anything, because every time I stepped on the mat, I defeated cerebral palsy, and I made a positive impact on people in the process. For a split second, I had wished that I could wrestle like everyone else. Not anymore! I made a declaration to myself that I was going to work harder than I ever had before! I was going to come back next year stronger and more flexible than the previous year. Cerebral palsy was not going to get the best of me!

The End of an Era - March 2013

I woke up early one crisp spring morning to a text from Coach Barnes, saying to meet him in his room for a team meeting. The excitement in me bubbled as I began to ponder what he might want to talk about. Dominick was the only one who made it to State this year, so maybe it was a new game plan on how we could improve our stats. Or it could be new procedure for next year.

I walked into Coach Barnes's room to find him sitting at his computer desk. He greeted me as I sat waiting for the others to arrive. Some time passed before he finally decided to start without the others. He began to tell me how proud he was of the team and of me. His tone then switched from optimistic to somber.

"I'm not sure what the future holds," he said.

"Why?" I asked.

Coach Barnes drew a deep breath and leaned back into his chair. "I'm resigning, Trevor."

My heart dropped into my stomach. My coach was leaving!

14

Return to Central Michigan

June 2013

A good name is to be more desired than great wealth, favor is better than silver and gold.

Proverbs 22:1 (NASB)

Day One

The news of Coach Barnes's resignation shook me to the core, but I had little time to dwell on it, because summer came in the blink of an eye. The opportunity presented itself and I decided to go back to Central Michigan University for their annual wrestling technique camp. I fell in love with the people there and couldn't wait to see everyone again.

Maybe Nate, Joey, and Luke will be there again, I thought.

My dad drove me up part of the way, and then my aunt and uncle drove me the rest of the way to campus. It was a very similar process compared to last time. I got weighed, registered, and shown to my room. I hadn't gained much weight since the season ended. I went from

126 lbs. to 128 lbs. in four months. The counselors from the camp last year seemed happy to see me back, and they even remembered I needed transportation to and from practice.

I walked into my room and began to unpack my stuff. I looked at the schedule for the week, and it too had a similar layout, including a tournament at the end of the week. It was some time before I heard the door open again, and in walked a tall, skinny kid with a buzz top haircut.

"Hi, my name is Cody Gappa," he introduced.

I introduced myself, and we began to talk. Cody was from the Upper Peninsula and drove four hours to get to CMU. Finally, he asked the question I had been waiting for.

"Do you mind if I ask you what's wrong with your legs?"

"I have cerebral palsy," I said. "My muscles are always really tight, and that's why I walk the way I do."

"Oh, okay. Do you go to church?" he asked.

"No, but I believe in God," I said.

"That's good," Cody said. "Always trust in God."

That was a strange conversation to have after you've explained your disability.

Soon after, the door opened again and in came a kid who was a little bit taller than me with spiky blonde hair. He introduced himself as J.R. and said he was from Indiana. Once we got our stuff unpacked, we headed off to the first session. I was excited to see Coach Borelli again.

Zach and CJ were back as well. I felt great during the first session, and I was able to keep pace with most of the people I wrestled with.

After the first session, Cody, J.R., and I really hit it off. We walked to 7-Eleven and talked about our lives.

"You're pretty strong and fast for someone with a disability," Cody said. He paused for a moment before adding, "I meant that in a good way."

"I know," I said with a smile. "I appreciate that."

While I genuinely appreciated his comment, I couldn't help but think that there is a long-standing stereotype that people with disabilities are not able to do the things that abled–bodied people can do. Adaptation may be necessary, but even the most disabled person can shatter expectations and break through barriers under the right motivation. Whether it be through self-advocacy or through another person advocating and rooting for their success.

Do not ever discredit even the smallest of victories. For example, the walk to 7-Eleven was not as tiring as it was the year before. That was proof I did as I said I would and came back stronger. As I laid down that night, I couldn't help but think about what the next season may bring. I won my first match during my freshman year, and I still had quite a bit of time left.

Day Two

The next morning, I woke up bursting with energy. The morning session was going to be referee's position, which meant I was going to get to introduce Cody and J.R. to the infamous cross face.

"Are you ready for practice?" Cody asked.

"Oh, yeah!" I said with cheerful determination.

Practice started, and it seemed like it took forever to get to the cross-face series. When Zach finally introduced it, I was like a kid on Christmas morning. I partnered up with Cody and J.R. once again and decided Cody was going to be my first victim. We both got into our positions and waited for the signal. Once the whistle blew, I rammed my forearm into Cody's nose.

"Oh, ouch!" Cody said, in his calm demeanor.

I knew I was in for it when it came to be Cody's turn. Cody came back and returned the favor with a cross face of his own right across my nose. I guess you could say I had it coming. J.R. and Cody switched out, and now it was J.R.'s turn to take a ride on the pain train. I reared back and nailed him as well.

"Are you trying to break my face?" he asked in surprise.

I laughed, "No, but if it happens, it happens."

The morning session ended, and I loaded up on the gator to ride back to campus. My driver was a beautiful young lady with brown hair and a gorgeous smile. On our way back, she asked me the question that, if I had a dollar for every time I had been asked that question within the past year, I'd be a millionaire.

"What do you want to do when you graduate?" she asked.

"I think I want to go into physical therapy," I said. It was the truth because I wanted to be able to help kids in similar situations I was in when I was younger.

Once we got back in the dorm, we hung out and ate lunch until it was time for the afternoon session. During this session, we worked on take downs from the standing (neutral) position. CJ demonstrated the tree top take down. He shot in like normal, hoisted Zach's leg up onto his shoulder, and threw him down to the mat. I was worried about doing this move, because I wasn't sure if I was going to be able to keep my balance. I partnered up with J.R. and decided to give it a shot. I shot in and was able to lift his leg just above my chest, but I started to lose my balance when I tried to lift it to my shoulder. I adapted and under–hooked the bottom half of his leg to accommodate my shoulder and threw him to the ground, just as CJ did.

The afternoon quickly turned to evening and, after the last session of the day, Cody, J.R., and I decided to go bowling. The big tournament was tomorrow, so what better way to celebrate than to not get any sleep. I hadn't bowled in years, and the last time I did, I had to use the assist ramp to roll the ball, because my balance wasn't good enough to roll it on my own. When it came to be my turn, I picked up the 14 lb. ball and hurled it down the lane. It lost momentum as it got closer to the pins, but I still took out five pins and ended the night with a score of 110. All without needing the ramp. Celebrate the little victories.

Day Three

To me, it's the most anticipated day of camp. The tournament was the place where I could test my mettle and determine how much I had improved. I didn't fare well the year prior, but this year was going to be different. I wasn't going to go down as easily. I made sure every single muscle fiber was as limber as it could be and headed out for my first match. We began wrestling, and I lasted two periods before finally getting pinned at the end of the second period. My second match came around, and I was able to go all three rounds without getting pinned. I lost, but I still gave them a fight. To me, that's all that mattered.

After the primary matches were over, I challenged J.R. to a match. J.R. was an Indiana semi-state qualifier. I wanted to see how well I would fare against him. To my delight, he gladly accepted. At the start of the match, we circled each other before J.R. scored a take down. I rolled onto my belly, quickly stood up and broke free from his grasp, granting me an escape point. We locked up just before J.R. took me down yet again. I fought to get back onto my hands and knees and was able to escape again just before the period ended. The score was now 4-2.

J.R. chose to go on bottom. When the whistle blew, J.R. quickly stood up and attempted to break the grip I had on his waist. Unable to do so, he ran toward the edge of the mat and pivoted with his hips. The momentum of the move caused me to break my grip and sent me flying out of bounds, almost landing on the mat next to ours. I quickly got up and charged after him. I was able to successfully grab one of his legs. At the same time, he placed me in a front headlock. Both of us were fighting with everything we had, but the second period ended before either one of us was able to get the advantage.

I was proud of myself, having made it to the third period with J.R. I positioned myself on top, and the referee blew the whistle. I blasted J.R. with a cross face, but he was able to duck underneath and get to his feet. In an attempt to get some points before time ran out, I grabbed his leg and desperately tried to get off my belly, so I could get around him. Unfortunately, time ran out before I could do anything, but J.R. wasn't able to score any more points either. At the end of the match, we shook each other's hands over a job well done.

That night, we spent our last night together, talking about everything under the sun. I laid down thinking about how it all goes by too quickly. Suddenly in the dark of night, I hear Cody's voice.

"Yeah, I had fun," Cody said, in between a yawn. "One thing is for sure, Trev…"

"What's that?" I asked.

"I'm never going to forget you."

Thomas and I receiving our varsity letters – March 2013

Sophomore Year
(10th Grade)

15

Everything's an Illusion

August 24th, 2013

"There is no footprint too small that it cannot leave an imprint on the world."

...we are of good courage, I say, and prefer rather to be absent from the body and to be at home with the Lord.

2 Corinthians 5:8 (NASB)

Just three days into the new school year, and I was already buzzing with excitement. I had already made some new friends and I couldn't wait to see what this year had in store. I made my way to history class and took my seat. Sitting directly behind me was none other than Brandon Wolfinger. Brandon is short in stature, standing barely above five feet, but definitely not on words. If he wanted to, he could talk your ear off all day.

Brandon and I were close in elementary school, but slowly drifted apart as we got older. It was nice to be able to catch up. We talked about the old days when we were younger and what kind of car we would get when we got our license. After class, we said our goodbyes and went our separate ways.

Later that night, as I was getting ready for bed, I was scrolling through social media when I came across a very cryptic post that read:

"This can't be real. Rest in peace, Brandon."

Frantic, I joined the thread to find out who it is. My heart dropped when I read the last name "Wolfinger." I had just talked to him that morning. He was his normal, happy-go-lucky self. Brandon can't really be dead, can he? Besides, we're only 15 or 16–years old; we are too young to die. To my dismay, I began to read post after post, confirming what I didn't want to be true. Brandon was out riding his bike, and he had gotten hit by a car.

The next morning, I met up with Aaron. I had known Aaron since my freshman year, but this was going to be the first time that we had met outside of school. Oh, how I wished it was under better circumstances. For a long while, we stood by his car and talked. I had the opportunity to meet his family, who seemed to be very nice people.

All of a sudden, I received a message on my phone saying there was going to be a memorial for Brandon at the high school. Aaron and I hopped in his car and raced over to see what it was all about. Upon getting there, my heart was shattered. It was a meeting for the soccer team that Brandon loved almost as much as life itself. The looks of pure sadness on his fellow teammates, his coaches, the principal, and even the super intendent was enough to make even the most hard-hearted person sob. It was a testament to just how much Brandon was truly loved.

The following Saturday, Brandon's Celebration of Life took place. As people began to pack in, I walked the line where they had pictures of Brandon and memorabilia displayed. Suddenly I stopped. Sitting on a staircase, in the middle of the stage, was an urn. An uneasy feeling came over me, knowing the remains of my friend were inside. It was a painful reminder of my own mortality.

I sat down beside Aaron as Brandon's godfather gave the eulogy. He spoke of many happy memories and jokes he had with Brandon, but what stuck out to me the most was the way he spoke about his positive spirit. Brandon lived every day wearing a smile on his face, spreading his infectious joy to everyone he met. Losing a classmate was a painful experience for me because I have very fond memories with so many of them. As I came face to face with my own mortality, I decided from that moment on, I was going to wrestle each match as if it were my last.

IN MEMORY OF BRANDON WOLFINGER

OCTOBER 7 1996 - AUGUST 24 2013

16

Redeemed

September 2013 – October 2013

that if you confess with your mouth the Lord Jesus and believe in your heart that God has raised Him from the dead, you will be saved.

Romans 10:9 (NKJV)

September 2013

I woke up out of a deep sleep to a text message from Aaron's stepfather, Shawn.

"Do you want to go to church with me this Sunday?"

I'm not sure why, but the few times I have stepped inside of a church, I always felt extremely uncomfortable. The services were always really boring, and the sermons put me to sleep. Despite my past experiences, I said yes. I woke up the next morning and immediately contemplated on changing my mind about attending church. I slowly got dressed and saw Shawn's pick-up truck pull in the driveway. There was no turning back now. After all, I did make a secret promise to God that if he let me get my license when I turned 16, I would start going to church.

I got in Shawn's truck, and he was smiling from ear to ear, and the music he was playing was different too. It wasn't Avenged

Sevenfold or Five Finger Death Punch. It was Jesus music and wasn't hymnal music either. It sounded like much of what you would hear in the modern age.

"This is David Crowder," Shawn said. The song that was playing was 'God Almighty, None Compares.' Followed by 'How He Loves.'

"Cool," I said sheepishly.

"I used to be a drunk, but Jesus came into my life and took it all away," Shawn said. "I don't even have the urge to drink anymore."

"That's awesome!" I said. *How could someone be hooked on alcohol, and one day, out of the blue, just quit?*

After about 20 minutes, we pulled into a gravel driveway. Out front read a sign: 'New Life Church.' From the moment I walked in the door, I was greeted by smiling people and handshakes. This was certainly different from any past experience I had at a church. The head pastor shook my hand and introduced himself as Pastor Tim McGinnis. I couldn't put my finger on it, but these people were different. I was about to open the door to the sanctuary before I was stopped by another older gentleman.

"Hi, my name is Pastor Bob," he said. The others seemed different, but this guy seemed very different. He was practically glowing with joy!

"I'm Trevor," I said.

"This guy is a wrestler," Shawn said.

"Oh!" Pastor Bob said, "Don't hurt me now."

I entered the sanctuary and saw the old wooden pews were replaced with cushioned chairs. There were no song books, but the words were projected on the screen. Instead of a lonely piano, there was an array of different instruments on stage. This was definitely not what I remembered growing up. The worship band began to play, and it wasn't old hymns they were singing but contemporary music. The energy was amazing! People were shouting and raising their hands, praising God.

As Pastor Tim was giving his message, one line he said made me more interested in a sermon then I had ever been.

"If I can stand up here every Sunday and faithfully preach the word to you with twenty-two cancerous tumors ravaging my body, what is stopping you from serving God?"

I couldn't get it out of my head. Twenty-two cancerous tumors and he was still faithfully preaching the Bible. What faith that man must have! Jesus isn't just someone I should believe to make it to Heaven, I should serve Him too.

October 2013

I continued to go to church with Aaron and his family for many weeks. I loved it each time I went and was getting to know all of the people there really well. I couldn't sleep one night, so I decided to do what every 15-year-old boy does and watch YouTube videos. As I was browsing, I came across this video titled, "I Know the Day of the Rapture." Intrigued, I clicked on the video.

I've always believed in God and the rapture, so I better see what this guy has to say.

He started out by introducing himself, and then went on to defend how he knew the day of the rapture.

"The rapture is going to happen in October of 2013," he began. "If you do not know Jesus Christ as your personal savior, you need to repent because time is running out. All you saints should be excited, but if you do not know Jesus, you should be very afraid. He is only coming for those who have truly repented and love Him. It is not enough just to believe in Jesus, you have to know Him as your personal savior if you want to make the rapture."

I paused the video and glanced at my calendar. It was indeed October of 2013. I hit play and listened to his instructions on how to receive Christ into my heart. That night in my bed, I repented of my sins and asked Christ into my heart. I wasn't quite sure what had just happened, but I do know one thing. The fear I had just moments ago was overtaken by a feeling of unbelievable peace.

Beyond the Mat

The Bible says that no man knows the day or the hour (Matthew 24:36). But God used the false teachings of a man and the belief in God I had already to bring me to Christ. He was right about one thing, however. I needed to be saved from my sins and have a personal relationship with Jesus Christ to get into Heaven before the rapture. It's not enough just to simply believe in God and hope we do enough good deeds to make it to Heaven. It is about a relationship with God.

The rapture might not have happened in October 2013, but trust me when I say it is very soon. The prophetic signs are coming together at a rate never before seen in the history of the world. If you don't have a personal relationship with Jesus Christ, now is the time to come to Him. Don't try to wait until it's too late. You don't have as much time left in this life as you think you do.

Beyond the Mat
Jake Daniels

When Trevor asked me to write this foreword, I struggled to find a specific thing to write about. There were numerous times that I was amazed by the determination he possessed. So, I finally decided to go with our introduction.

One hour and counting. I was starting to wonder just how long this kid was going to want to roll. He finally started to tire out after the hour-and-a-half mark, and we decided to call it a night. That was the first open mat that I had held at the new school I had just been hired at. The doors were open, the sun was shining and the spring breeze was blowing through the building. Man, the weather was nice out. I started to doubt myself for even holding the open mat. There's a great correlation of good weather to bad attendance for open mats in the spring.

Around five until the session was supposed to start, the first and only person showed up. I noticed out of the corner of my eye that this kid seemed to have tripped or something when walking into the building. Smiling, I focused in and could instantly tell this kid was ripped. Still recovering from his entrance into the building, he introduced himself and assured me he was okay. He then replied that him stumbling around "happens all the time," and I came to realize that this young man was working with some adversity.

Trevor was the only wrestler to show up that night. We talked for a bit and got to know each other somewhat. We talked about his age, grade, and previous wrestling accomplishments. Then I found out that he had only won one match, and that was against a girl. With that being said, I suggested it was time to get to work. Trevor didn't blink an eye. We started off with agilities and some basic fundamentals when it comes to pre-practice for wrestling. He struggled but didn't give me one excuse or reason for his trouble. I decided to see what his wrestling skill was like.

We went one-on-one for about an hour and half. I weighed about 270-280 pounds at the time, and this young man was 120-130 soaking wet. Little did I know this would be the first of many goes with this kid. It didn't matter how bad he lost, he just kept coming. Eventually as the session went on, we would drill certain technique with Trevor. He was like a sponge. Every word I said he mimicked, especially what I told him about the infamous cross face. Finally, it was time to call it a day, even though Trevor didn't want to. I assured him that there would be plenty of time to get better.

The next three years would be filled with adaptations to his technique to make him as competitive as possible. He accepted any and all advice when it came to wrestling, school, and life. It didn't matter how hard I was on the team; Trevor was a model for overcoming adversity.

Jake Daniels

Logan Elm High School wrestling coach

2013 - present

17

Pushed to the Limit

November 2013 – December 2013

I can do all things through Christ who strengthens me.

Philippians 4:13 (NKJV)

November 2013

Another season reared its head, and I was eager to see how this new coach would do. He wasn't from the Logan Elm area. The only thing I knew about him was that he was excited to be coming. Before practice started, he introduced himself and the assistant coaches.

"My name is Coach Daniels," he began. "I'm not going to be easy on you guys. This is a sport that separates the men from the boys. You'll be here at practice and for every practice you miss, it's ten bear crawls. You'll make weight during the week of a tournament. On Monday, you're allowed to be eight pounds over your allotted weight class. On Tuesday, six pounds. On Wednesday, four pounds. On Thursday, two pounds. On Friday, you better be on weight. If you are not on weight during any one of those days, it's one bear crawl for every tenth of a pound you're over. This isn't to punish you, but to teach you discipline."

The assistant coaches' names were Coach Wolford and Coach Dietrich. They seemed much more laid back than Coach Daniels. I looked over at the clock; there was about one minute left in our warm-up jog when Coach Daniels called out.

"Pick it up, 80%." I did as he said and set a quicker pace. Thirty seconds later, Coach Daniels called out again.

"90%, run faster." I echoed his command and took off in a full run. Twenty seconds later, he cried out once again.

"100%. Sprint, give it everything you got." I ran as fast as my legs would carry me until the timer hit zero.

We moved into agilities. I was still unable to do most of them but didn't dwell on it. Coach Daniels gave us a series of moves to drill. We drilled for five minutes before he called us into a circle. Like always, since it was the first day of practice, we reviewed the basics. I was becoming well versed in the sport and was helping the less experienced wrestlers in their craft. As we were drilling the new moves, Coach Daniels called out again.

"Everybody get on the wall," he said. We all hurried over, curious as to what he was going to have us do next. "Stay with your drilling partner," he said. "You've got ten minutes to do 20 bear crawls. You're going to sprint down and bear crawl back. Down and back is one."

Dominick took off like a cheetah and was down and back in no time. My turn came, and I sprinted as fast as I could down to the other end of the mat. I was much slower than your average sprinter but knew I could probably make up for it when doing the bear crawl. It didn't turn out like I had hoped. I could do the bear crawl but couldn't use both of my arms at the same time to propel myself faster. I had to move one limb at a time. This, in turn, slowed Dominick and me down significantly. So much so, we didn't even finish before the time ran out.

After we finished the bear crawls, we moved into sessions of live wrestling. We did ten straight rounds of live wrestling before Coach Daniels called us into a circle around the mat. He called DJ to the center and explained what we were going to do.

"At the end of every practice from now on, you will be doing up-downs (grass drills)," Coach Daniels said. "The leader is whoever I decide will be in the middle. They will decide how many up-downs you do at the end of practice. The only condition is for every up-down you do, you have to add another one on the next day. For example, if DJ decides to do ten up-downs today, you'll have to do eleven tomorrow, and so on."

As it turns out, DJ did, in fact, make us do ten up-downs. Unbeknownst to us, he would come to regret that decision later. If this first practice was any indication, Coach Daniel's practices were much harder than Coach Barnes's or Coach Polly's. They even rivaled Coach Polly's "wear 'em out Wednesday" practices, and it wasn't even Wednesday.

Casper the Ghost- December 2013

The season was well under-way and I wished I could tell you I had gone undefeated and was ranked #1 in the nation, but that was not the case. In fact, I was probably doing the worst I'd ever done in my entire career. To top it all off, the team as a whole did awful during our last meet. We didn't even place in the top five. Which could only mean one thing: We were about to feel the wrath of Coach Daniels.

Everyone was on edge. We all knew the consequences of a poor performance. Tensions continued to mount as Coach Daniels casually greeted us in the locker room.

"Hey, fellas," he said.

He walked outside as we waited for a bellowing yell to tell us to get moving, but it never came. We had another wrestling meet coming up, so we needed to do wrestle-offs. As we finished our warm-up jog, we gathered in a circle to watch the matches.

"What are you doing?" Coach Daniels growled. "Keep running, only those who are wrestling should be on the inside of the mat." We ran for an additional ten minutes as those who had to wrestle off completed their matches.

As was the norm for the first practice after a meet, Coach Daniels critiqued us on what we could do better. Nothing out of the ordinary yet, but you could sense a heavy tension in the air. We did ten rounds of one-minute drills before it came to a sudden stop.

"Get jogging," Coach Daniels said.

We trotted around the room for about a minute before Coach Daniels yelled out again.

"Sprint!" he yelled.

I bolted around the room as fast as I could until Coach Daniels told us to start jogging again. We did this sprint-jog sequence a total of five times. By the last go around, my chest was on fire, and it took all I had to manage short, shallow breaths. I stumbled over and hugged the water fountain as I brought life's nectar to my lips. We gathered around as Coach Daniels began to teach on the referee's position.

"This is called the post-throw," Coach Daniels began. "When you have your opponent down flat, you're going to keep him from posting by clearing his elbow. After that, you're going to throw in the cross face. Once you have the cross face, you're going to keep hold of his arm, bring his head to his knees, and lock in the cradle."

This is perfect for me! I may have finally found my bread-and-butter move.

I practiced the move on my partner, and it worked flawlessly. We worked on a few more moves from the referee's position before Coach Daniels called us over to the wall.

"You got ten minutes to do twenty bear crawls," he said.

When it was my turn, to make up for lost time, I would sprint the whole way. I still got a great workout in even if I wasn't doing the exact same thing as everyone else. From there, we went straight into live wrestling with barely enough time to catch our breath. At this point, my entire body ached, and I struggled for breath but continued to press on. After ten straight rounds of live wrestling, Coach Daniels called us back over to the wall.

"We're going to do a few suicides, and then you'll be done," he said.

I ran as hard and as fast as I could. As I was finishing my last sprint, my muscles began to cramp up, but I pushed through and finished. Afterward, I joined the others in the middle of the circle. We still had up-downs to do, and at this point in the year, we were over thirty. This was by far the hardest practice we've ever had. During the up-downs, I began to feel strange. My heart rate wasn't coming down and my arms began to feel heavy and tingly. After the team huddle, I stumbled into the locker room and folded into the chair.

"Are you okay, Trev?" Dominick asked.

I tried to say something, but I couldn't form the words. The next thing I knew, I was being carried outside. The squad came, and an EMT handed me a tube of glucose. I had passed out from pure exhaustion. A few minutes, later my dad walked in with a puzzled look on his face.

"What's going on?" he asked.

"We just got paid a visit from Casper, the white Ghost," Coach Daniels said.

All's Fair in Love and War

In the sport of wrestling, anything that can happen, usually does. From all-out brawls, having accidents on the mat, fans getting kicked out of the gym for being obnoxious, and even teammates having to wrestle each other in a tournament match. The diversity of wrestling is what makes the sport so great. Our next meet was at Madison Plains, which also just so happened to be Coach Daniel's alma mater. As is always the case, you never know who or what you're going up against until the day of the tournament. However, I did know that my bracket was small, so there was a good chance I could win a match or even place in the tournament.

I waited with great anticipation as to who I was going to wrestle first. I could hardly contain my excitement when I saw Coach Daniels with the bout sheets in hand.

"You're going to wrestle Trevor Grambo in your first match," Coach Daniels said.

Awesome! Wait… what? Trevor is on the same wrestling team that I am, and I'm going to have to wrestle him?

My bout number came up, and sure enough, I was going to wrestle Trevor Grambo in my first match. The match started, and we laughed as we circled each other, waiting for the other to make a move. I glanced over at Coach Daniels, who did not look amused in the slightest. I dove for Grambo's leg to try to take him down. I wrestled with him a lot during practice, so he knew me well. He had me rolled up and pinned in the first period. I wasn't upset about it. In fact, I still found it quite funny after the match was over.

After about an hour wait, my next match was about to start. I scanned the bracket to see who I was going to wrestle next. My next opponent was… Dominick? I had to wrestle my own teammate not once, but twice. I took Dominick a little more seriously because I knew he was in it to win it.

"You're going down," Dominick joked.

The ref started the match and I was able to fight Dominick off for about 45 seconds before he rolled me up for the pin. With that match, I was done for the day, but because my bracket was so small, I earned my very first medal at a tournament. I was probably the happiest person that ever placed 5th at a tournament. To wrestle and actually earn this medal was something I was extremely proud of and was determined to earn more with even higher prestige.

Junior Year (11th Grade)

Beyond the Mat

Ken Wilson

In 2014-15 I get a message from some kid. I had never met him before, and I really didn't want to based on the question he asked me! It was a question about sin, of which I am well versed, but he caught me off guard. For the first time in my life, I was speechless! And I'm a Pastor and professional wrestler!

At first, I tried to ignore him. I told him to take a hike (kidding!). But, if you know Trevor, you know that he is tenacious and doesn't give up, so I answered his question. I first told him that he was destined for hell (again, kidding!). But I gave him some pointers and from that point on, we became great friends. I began mentoring a small-town boy from Circleville, Ohio – or from my point of view, Redneckville.

As he continued to grow in the Lord, I saw a love for others grow in him. Most importantly, I saw Jesus in him 24/7. He has a passion to serve our God and the disabled in his sphere of influence. Trevor has a heart for the lost no matter if they are disabled or able bodied. He had dreams of being a pro wrestler but has surrendered to the will of God and at such a young age!

He was 16 when we met and has done more than most Pastors in their 40s. You will find that out as you read the rest of this book! Trevor has truly blessed an old fat guy like me! I think I am his mentor when in reality, it is a two-way street!

Trevor, thank you for being a friend to Julia and I. We love you like a son!

Lord, Father God,

Bless Trevor and the ministry you have called him to do -- to serve and win souls. And that the Holy spirit would Baptize him with fire! Agape and in Jesus name, Amen!

Lord Rev. Ken and Julia Wilson.

18

The Power of Social Media

October 2014

Iron sharpens iron, so one man sharpens another.

Proverbs 27:17 (NASB)

There tends to be a negative vibe that is felt whenever you say you've met someone online. There are very real dangers of talking to someone online, but meeting people online doesn't always equate to a dangerous situation. As a matter of fact, social media can be used as a powerful tool to uplift and inspire others. One day, the Lord led me to post my testimony on many faith-based groups I was a part of on Facebook. I received dozens upon dozens of responses, but one response in particular, caught my eye.

In my testimony, I mentioned my dream was to become a professional wrestler. A man had commented on one of my posts, saying that he was a professional wrestler who was a follower of Jesus, and he knew a lot of famous wrestlers who were Christians. I immediately friended him, thinking that I could pick his brain about other wrestlers he knew and how to get into the business. His name was Ken Wilson. We didn't talk to one another for a while, until one day I mustered up the courage to ask him a faith-related question.

"You should save those kinds of questions for your pastor," he replied.

I could see that he wasn't interested in talking, so I just left well enough alone. A few days later, I got a surprising message from Ken that read:

"I'm sorry about my response. I didn't mean to come off as rude. Judging by your testimony, God has great plans for your life!"

We hit it off ever since that day. Ken even began to mentor me in the Word and help me understand many biblical principles. Ken continued to bless me in many ways with his wisdom, but he never failed to tell me that I was a blessing to him as well. Ken told me he had a chronic condition called lymphedema. It is a painful condition where your lymphatic system backs up and is not able to eliminate waste from the blood. This causes painful swelling in the affected areas.

"Seeing how you go through cerebral palsy, and still serve the Lord with a smile on your face, blesses me like you wouldn't believe," Ken said. "You give me the courage to face my own disability."

"I've never looked at my disability as a burden," I said. "It's always been a blessing."

Over the next few months, I watched as Ken had many extended hospital stays, went through a financial crisis, and had many people turn on him because of his faith. Through all of that, his faith in

God never wavered. That's what I admired most about Ken. Even when he was at rock bottom, he knew that his God was bigger than any problem he could ever face. We fed off one another and carried each other's burdens, just as the Bible says to do. He was the best spiritual mentor anyone could have.

Beyond the Mat

Like Ken, you might be going through a windstorm of trials. It could be you are battling with your own disability or financial trouble. Maybe someone has turned his back on you, and you feel all alone. I want to encourage you to look at your challenges from God's perspective. 2 Corinthians 12:10 instructs us to find pleasure or to give God glory even in our sufferings. In John 9, when Jesus encounters the blind man, His disciples ask Him, ""Rabbi, who sinned, this man or his parents, that he was born blind?" Jesus answered, "It was not that this man sinned, or his parents, but that the works of God might be displayed in him."

After their conversation, Jesus then goes on to heal the blind man. This miracle of healing could not have taken place if the man was not blind. In other words, Jesus's power could not have been shown in such a mighty way if the man was not born blind. Like this man's blindness, your challenges or handicaps are a window for God's mightiest works to be shown in you.

19

Casper the Ghost Returns

January 2015

Nevertheless, you have done well to share with me in my affliction.

Philippians 4:14 (NASB)

My junior year was off to a fantastic start. I may have not had much success individually, having still remained winless since freshman year, but the team was doing better than ever. We won first place in the first three tournaments of the year before falling to runner-up in the fourth meet. Seeing our rapid success, Coach Daniels began to make our practices even harder and longer. Practices began at 3:00 PM and ended at 6:00 PM with an hour of weightlifting and two hours of practice. If you missed practice, instead of ten bear crawls, it was 100. I understand why he started pushing us so hard, though. Coach Daniels saw how much we improved from the previous year and wanted to help us reach our full potential.

    I mentioned earlier how wrestlers like to frequently pull pranks on one another, and I was not exempt from being a victim. Once, while lacing up my shoes, getting ready for practice my hood from my hoodie was suddenly pulled over my head. A few seconds later, my arms began to come out of their sleeves against their will. With my eyes blinded and my arms immobilized, the bandits took it one step further and duct-taped my legs together. The next thing I knew, my helpless body was being carried by a sea of laughing wrestlers. I was sat upon a bench where I received the tickling of a lifetime. I was helpless to defend myself. All I could do was wait out the storm. They had their fun and untied my hands and ripped the duct tape off my legs. Let's face it, I had fun too. When I could see again, I discovered the culprits were DJ, Chase, and Dominick.

Coach Daniels came out of his office, which meant we had better start running. He added a twist to our warm-up. In addition to our run, while the others were running, we had to include three sets of ten pull-ups and climb the rope three times. After the ten minutes were up, we moved to agilities. This was the one area I still had not made any improvement in, but I didn't give up hope.

"We're going to go hard today, fellas," Coach Daniels said.

You could feel the tension build in the room. We began drilling like normal, except this time, we did ten rounds of drilling instead of five. Afterward, Coach Daniels pulled us off to the side and demonstrated moves we needed to improve on. We drilled those for a few minutes before we heard those dreaded three words.

"On the wall," Coach Daniels called out.

Every time I heard him say those words, a chill ran down my spine.

"Sprint down and army crawl back," he said.

I took off as fast as I could down the mat and quickly hit the floor to army crawl back. Since we weren't allowed to use our legs in this exercise, I didn't have to worry about slowing everybody else down. In fact, I even beat a few people back to the starting line. I noticed something else as well; I wasn't getting tired as quickly as I used to. The practices might be difficult, but I was reaping the benefits of Coach Daniels being so hard on us. The best part was that I finished around the same time as everyone else.

From there, we wrestled more live drills. Coach Daniels wasn't kidding when he said this practice was going to be harder than usual. With each new round, the fatigue on my muscles grew. I was praying for a break but instead, Coach Daniels said, "Get jogging."

"Get jogging." We all were showing signs of fatigue, jogging at a snail's pace.

"Who's going to be a leader in here, boys?" Coach Daniels asked. "It's all about mental toughness. Now sprint!"

I took off like a bolt of lightning, if lightning was filmed in slow motion, that is. I was tired but was doing the best I could. We repeated this sequence five times before going back into live wrestling. Never in my life had I been pushed this hard. Coach Daniels set the timer for twenty minutes and we transitioned into drilling.

"Whatever move I call out is the move you hit," Coach Daniels said. "One guy hits it, and then the other guy goes."

One after another, Coach Daniels named every takedown we had ever drilled. As tired as I was, I still managed to hit every one of them. The twenty-minute time crawled slowly to 0, but our suffering was not over.

"Get on the wall," Coach Daniels said. "Give me five good suicides, and then you're done."

At this point, it took everything I had just to stay on my feet. Despite being weak at the knees, I continued forward and completed all five suicides. Just when I thought it was over, Coach Daniels spoke up again.

"Whoops, overtime. Give me three extra suicides. It's all about mental toughness, fellas," he repeated.

Reluctantly, we all completed the extra suicides, which added up to a grand total of eight. Practice wasn't over quite yet. We still had to do our up-downs, and, at this point in the season, we were up to 47. It just so happened that Coach Daniels picked me to lead the team at the end. Even though I was more tired than I ever had been, I was still determined to finish strong. I did okay up until 30. After that, I felt my heart rate begin to quicken and a pins-and-needles feeling in my fingers.

"Come on, let's go! Finish strong!" DJ said, sensing I was starting to slow down. I could tell my teammates didn't care how slow I was going, but they did want to make sure I got all of the up-downs done.

By some miracle, I managed to do all of the up-downs. However, the battle wasn't over. I still had to lead the team in jumping jacks. I stood up, my skin felt clammy, and my vision became blurry, but I at least wanted to finish the practice before I passed out. I managed to finish the jumping jacks without completely passing out, but Dominick and DJ still had to carry me over to a chair, because I was too weak to hold myself up.

"We're going to do this again, huh?" Coach Daniels said.

"What happened this time?" Dad asked.

"Casper, the white ghost, paid us a visit again," Coach Daniels said.

Cerebral palsy may cause me to use a lot more energy than most, but that wasn't going to stop me. After I got some fluids, I was as good as new and ready to go back at it again the next day.

Beyond the Mat

Sometimes, life will beat you up so badly, you'll feel as if you're on the verge of collapsing. I certainly was at the end of the hardest practice of my life. I was in and out of consciousness while doing the mat drills, and I was only able to finish through sheer willpower and the support of my teammates. I started to fall, but my teammates caught me before I could hit the floor. You might be in a place where you feel like you're going to collapse. You've been pushed to the limit, and nothing is going right for you. To make matters worse, you feel like you're all alone.

You are not alone. You are loved by more people than you realize. Keep going, and don't give up. There is always someone there to catch you when you fall (Psalm 37:24, 118:13).

20

A Ride to Remember

January 2015

You have established all the boundaries of the earth; You have made summer and winter.

Psalms 74:17 (NASB)

A bitterly cold wind attacked my face as I made my way to my car. It was a Saturday morning in January, which meant a wrestling tournament was sure to take place. We were heading to Milton Union, which is a two-hour bus ride from Logan Elm. I would be able to catch up on lost sleep. As I got closer to the school, the temperature continued to drop. By the time I arrived, the temperature was a frigid -2 degrees Fahrenheit. I hurried inside the wrestling barn to join my teammates and wait for the bus to arrive.

Time passed, and the bus was nowhere to be found. With the ride to Milton Union being two hours, Coach Daniels was getting worried. The bus finally arrived just in time so that we wouldn't be late. I shuffled my way to the bus, dodging patches of ice in my path. Cerebral palsy and ice don't mix. I boarded the bus, looking forward to feeling the warmth of the heater as I settled in for a pre-match nap.

This is what typically would happen, except this time I was met with a blast of even colder air.

"Can we turn on the heat?" DJ asked.

"I'm sorry," the bus driver said. "The heater is broken."

Oh, great!

I hobbled my way to my seat and sat down to try to get warm. One of the challenges of cerebral palsy is the inability to tolerate colder weather. The freezing temperatures cause the muscles to tighten up even more, making it difficult to move. As we began to hit the road, it got even colder. I frantically looked for the source of this arctic blast hovering over me when I spotted a window, about a third of the way open, in front of me.

This bus driver must be insane, leaving the windows down in the dead of winter.

I crawled over to the seat to put up the window. Try as I might, the latches weren't budging. I tried to push it up, but it wouldn't work.

"I'm sorry," the bus driver spoke up. "About half of the windows on this bus are broken and won't latch."

I slumped back into my seat and prepared myself for a long ride. Coach Dietrich was sitting in the seat adjacent to mine. I looked over, and all I could see were his eyes. He was covered from head to toe in scarves, hats, and winter coats. He looked like an Eskimo! After a grueling, two-hour ride, we arrived at the school. I tried to stand up, but couldn't. My legs were weak, and my feet felt heavy and numb. I was elated when I stepped inside the building and felt a warm rush of air come over me. It took almost an hour for me to get completely warm.

With that ordeal out of the way, it was time to get down to business. My first match of the day was against a kid from Milton Union. We began the match, and about twenty seconds in, he took me down and put me in a double chicken wing pin combo. As the referee began the count, I scrambled for a way to get out. Finally, I bridged up on my neck to prevent my shoulders from touching the mat. This strategy helped me advance to the second period. I was forced to go to the bottom position, while my opponent chose to take top. I tried to sit out and get a reversal, but my opponent was quicker than me. He balled me up into a cradle at the beginning of the second period.

It was a double-elimination style tournament, which meant I had one more chance to advance. If you don't know by now, I am never one to simply lay down for anybody I wrestle. The next kid I wrestled was able to take me down and keep me down for most of the match. However, he had to go through all three periods to win. I didn't get to wrestle much during the tournament, but I did get to watch Thomas get 2nd place in his weight class, and we as a team, won the whole tournament.

Afterward, Thomas and I crammed in between my younger brother in my parent's car. There was no way that we were going to ride the polar school bus again. We joked about our younger days, and Thomas would never let me live it down about the time I called him Lommy. In the midst of all the reminiscing, we each came to the realization that we only had one more year left to do this.

Beyond the Mat

Life really does fly by. Eleven years had gone by since my famous slip of the tongue, but it felt like just a few weeks. Furthermore, five of the six years of my wrestling career were gone. The Bible says that life is just like a vapor. It appears for a moment but then vanishes. On the bus ride of life, millions of people are constantly preparing for the next destination. It could be graduating high school or college, getting married, having kids, or acquiring as much wealth as possible. After you accomplish your goals, you deposit 50 cents, you get on the next, and the next, and so on.

Your goals are being met, and life is going well, but while you've been busy with life, you've been ignoring the signs that the bus fee is going to increase from 50 cents to 55 cents. Just as you are about to board the bus with the sign flashing, 'Destination: Heaven', you deposit your 50 cents and begin to walk up the steps.

"Hold on there, son," the bus driver says. "You're a nickel short. I'm afraid I can't let you on."

"Can't you make an exception?"

"I'm afraid not. You must have the fee paid in full before I can let you on. I'm going to have to ask you to step off."

You step off the bus in disbelief, because you thought you did everything right to be able to get on the bus. You then become angry because no one told you that the fee was going to increase, when, in fact, the signs were posted all around you, warning you of the price change. The driver even announced the price change over the loud speaker, but you were unable to hear, because you had your noise-canceling headphones on. Worse still, you weren't just warned on your last bus ride. You were being warned on every bus you had ever taken throughout your life, but you didn't listen.

When we stand before God, we are going to give an account for everything we've done with our lives. At the end of our lives, it's not going to matter how successful we were or how much money we had. All that will matter is if we had a personal relationship with Jesus Christ. We could never get to Heaven on our own; Jesus paid the fee of our sins in full so we could live with Him forever in Heaven.

So often, we try to pay the fee ourselves by being a good person or trying to be as successful as possible. However, if we try to get in that way, we will always come up one nickel short. The train ride to follow will be a direct contrast to the bus ride I just described. Christ paid the penalty for your sin on the cross so that we can come into a relationship with Him.

All you have to do is repent of your sins and ask Christ into your heart. God is always sending people to preach and warn of the coming judgement and the consequences of not following Christ. The signs are posted all around you. Are you listening?

21

Lights! Camera! Action!

February 2015

And they overcame him by the blood of the Lamb, and by the word of their testimony…

Revelation 12:11 (KJV)

Winters in Ohio are unpredictable, to say the least. It can be 50 degrees Fahrenheit and sunny one day and then drop to subzero temperatures the next. In rural southern Ohio, the slightest dusting of snow can cause the whole county to shut down. As it was in this case. Logan Elm had been closed for a week due to heavy snowfall and extreme cold. Five inches of snow blanketed the ground, and the windchill was a frosty -40 degrees Fahrenheit.

After a while, it's almost impossible to not go stir crazy being cooped up inside. The good news is we still had wrestling practice. Before practice, I laid on my bed, scrolling through my phone when I got a text from Coach Daniels.

"You're getting interviewed. Pick somebody from the team who you want to be interviewed with."

"Interviewed? By who?" I answered back.

"Kristyn Hartman, from 10TV news," Coach Daniels said.

I couldn't believe it. I was going to get to share my story on the news! I had seen other people with disabilities share their stories of overcoming the odds, and now I was going to get that chance as well. However, I was faced with a dilemma. It was going to be impossible for me to pick just one person to interview with when the entire team meant so much to me.

"Do you want to have the whole team be a part of it?" Coach Daniels asked. To which I responded with a resounding, "Yes!"

With my excitement at a boiling point, I hopped in my car and headed over to the wrestling barn. The interview was scheduled for Thursday, in just two short days. Before that, we had a scrimmage. We all hopped in the van and headed for Amanda Clear-creek High School.

"I can't believe you're going to be on TV, Trev," Garrett said.

"Are you nervous?" Nick asked.

I had to admit, I was a little nervous. I had never been on TV before. This was going to be seen by thousands of people. What if I messed up? We arrived at the school, and I got dressed and ready for practice. Word began to spread quickly about my TV interview, and some of the Amanda wrestlers were excited for me as well. I was making my rounds, jogging when the Amanda wrestling coach stopped me.

"Congratulations, son," he said. "You're a real inspiration. I've watched you year after year. It seems like you've been around this sport forever."

He was right, it did seem like a long time. Time seemed to be crawling, yet flying, by all at the same time. Five years couldn't go by that quickly, could it? After practice, I got changed and heard my phone kept going off. I made the announcement on social media that I was going to be interviewed by 10TV. The response was unreal. Hundreds of people were congratulating me and wishing me luck. It made me realize that we touch a lot more people than we could ever know.

The day of the interview finally arrived. The interview was scheduled to take place right after school, and I could hardly contain my excitement. The student body seemed to be in the same boat. I had people stopping me in the hall to wish me luck, and the teachers and staff seemed to be excited as well. At lunch, some of my friends made some rather off-color suggestions as to how I should answer the questions I get asked. I was about to shrug them off when suddenly, I saw Coach Daniels heading my direction.

"10TV called," he said. "They have rescheduled your interview for Monday."

My heart sank. I was ready to do the interview now, but at least they didn't completely cancel it. Monday couldn't come soon enough, and when it finally did, I could hardly contain myself. The interview was scheduled to take place during the lunch period this time around, and there was no phone call indicating they were going to reschedule it. I sat in the office with Coach Daniels, waiting with unhinged anticipation for the news crew to arrive. The sectional tournament was also this upcoming weekend, which made it all the sweeter. As we waited, the time for their scheduled arrival passed. Ten minutes, and then twenty minutes, then thirty, then forty minutes passed. It was apparent that they weren't coming.

I was devastated. Had they forgotten, or did they not want to do it anymore? Coach Daniels promised me that he would get to the bottom of the situation, but I still left with my head hung low. Later that night, my phone pinged. It was a text message from Coach Daniels.

"Your interview will be taking place tomorrow," he said.

I was excited, but I was also afraid of the forecasted snow. We were supposed to be getting over three inches of snow that night, which meant that Logan Elm would close for sure. The next morning, I woke up, and Logan Elm had closed. I looked outside and was greeted by a sea of white, fluffy snow. Surely, the interview was going to be canceled again. A few minutes later, I received a mass text from Coach Daniels, which read:

"Be at the barn at 1:00 for Trevor's interview."

It was finally happening! I raced to the car and quickly drove over to the wrestling barn. My excitement was building, but in the back of my mind, I was anticipating the interview being canceled again. My anxiety turned to delight as I saw the news van sitting in the parking lot when I pulled in. The camera crew was still preparing when I walked in, but there was no sign of the news reporter. There, with the camera crew, was a tall woman with beautiful, medium length blonde hair and a smile that could light up a room. I instantly recognized her as Kristyn Hartman.

"You must be Trevor," Kristyn said, with her signature smile. "We'd like to interview you after we get some footage.

"Yeah, sure." I said.

We started our warm-up jog, and just as I was rounding the first bend, my mother walked in. Shortly afterward, the high school principal, Mr. Smith, made an appearance. We ran it like a regular practice, but with cameras everywhere. After some drills and a quick cardio session, it was finally time to do the interview. I sat directly across from Kristyn, with my heart beating a mile a minute.

"So, Trevor," Kristyn began. "You're a pretty remarkable kid."

"I try," I said bashfully.

"Describe to me what the beginning of your life was like," Kristyn asked. "You had some pretty serious challenges."

I began to share with her about my birth. How I was born four months early, and the doctors said I would never survive, let alone walk. I shared with her all of the challenges I had in the first five years of my life and explained how the community of Circleville rallied behind me to make sure I had everything I needed to succeed.

"Where does wrestling come into the picture?" she asked.

"I started wrestling in 7th grade," I said. "Mainly because I am a huge professional wrestling fan, and this is the closest thing I could get to pro wrestling at the time." I paused for a second before continuing. "But, it's about so much more than that now."

"Have you ever won a match?" she asked.

"I've only won one match," I said.

"What was that experience like?"

"It was unreal!" I said. "People were jumping up and down and screaming and wrestlers from other teams were cheering for me. I had never heard a gym come unglued like that! It was indescribable!" I recalled.

"Going off of that," she began. "You mentioned you only won one match which means you've lost every other match. Losing can be hard for some; how do you handle the process of losing?"

"When it comes to losing, I guess you could say that I've gotten used to it." I said. "My body works differently than others which makes it more difficult to move the same way everyone else does. Don't get me wrong, losing still sucks at times, and I want to win, but at the same time, it's just as rewarding to see someone inspired by how hard you work."

Kristyn leaned back in her chair and smiled. "One last question," she said. "What does your shirt say?"

"If it doesn't challenge you, it doesn't change you." I read aloud.

"Isn't that like your life?" she asked.

"In a nutshell, yeah," I laughed.

The interview concluded, and they asked each of my teammates to describe me in one word. My heart was touched as they used words like dedicated, determined, resilient, and inspiring.

National Sensation

The interview aired on the day before sectionals and the response was overwhelming. I was receiving messages from people all over the United States about how people were being touched by my story or how I was helping them overcome a battle in their own lives. I got reports that my story was being featured as far east as New York, as far west as California, and as far south as Florida. I couldn't believe I was touching so many people!

The day of sectionals finally arrived. Fresh off the TV interview, I was fired up and ready to go! As I found my seat on the bus, a sobering thought crossed my mind. I came to the realization that I only have one more year to do this. I was woken out of my deep train of thought by the sound of Dominick's voice.

"Trev, your interview is going viral," Dom exclaimed.

"I saw that," I said.

"So much so that ESPN may want to do a story on you!" he said.

I looked at him in disbelief and couldn't believe it had traveled so far. I couldn't let the possibility distract me, though. My first match of the night was against the previous year's state champion, and I couldn't afford any distractions. The moments leading up to my match were "standard protocol," if you will. The butterflies in my stomach were fluttering as I pondered the magnitude of my opponent instead of focusing on wrestling the match. Many times, in life, we ponder how big our circumstances are instead of focusing on how big our God is. We then tend to judge God based upon our circumstances, instead of judging our circumstances based upon God.

I stepped onto the mat and faced a person who looked as if he were carved out of stone. The match began, and we locked up. Locking up with Kelly, it was as if I was wrestling a bear. I tried desperately to grab onto one of his legs, but it was like trying to grab ahold of a tree trunk. I managed to grab his thigh, but he easily shook me off. In a flash, he spun around me, got the takedown, and had me on my back before I could even react. There was a reason he placed first at state the previous year. I ended up losing that match in less than a minute, but it was still a fun experience. I had a bye the next round, which meant that I would have to wait until the next day to wrestle again.

The night seemed to crawl, but eventually, morning did come again. This was the last chance I would have to go to districts this year. My mom came and sat beside me while I was watching the other matches play out and delivered news that completely rocked my world.

"Ellen DeGeneres called the school and was wondering if you would be interested in being on her show," mom said.

At first, I thought she was lying, but she assured me that she was serious. That motivated me all the more to wrestle the best match ever. I walked onto the mat with increased confidence and bravado only to get squashed in thirty seconds. My junior season was over. I had no time to dwell on the quick loss, because it was time to get ready for my final season, and I was determined to make it my best.

We tried for weeks to get ahold of Ellen DeGeneres and ESPN again but to no avail. It was difficult to hide my disappointment having lost such a great opportunity, but I was driving home one day when The Lord spoke to me and said, "Don't worry, I have something much better in mind."

Beyond the Mat

- I'm sure we've all been there. The opportunity of a lifetime comes along, but it suddenly falls through. Don't be discouraged. Often, an opportunity will come along that benefits this life but not the next. God has your eternal best interest at heart.
- Never be afraid to share your story. You never know who is listening.

Wrestling Austin Shannon at Logan Elm

Doggy pile on Micha!

Sectional Championship 2015

Receiving the Sportsmanship, Ethics and Integrity award

12th Grade (Senior Year)

22

The First of Many Last Times

June 2015

that is, that I may be encouraged together with you by the mutual faith both of you and me.

Romans 1:12

Summer reared its head once again. The arrival of June signaled it was time to embark on my yearly tradition of attending Central Michigan University's wrestling technique camp. The process was very similar to every year prior. I packed a week's worth of clothes and set out on the five-hour journey with my aunt and uncle. When we arrived, I walked into the training facility, and instantly something felt different. A lot of the volunteers that were there with me in the beginning had long since graduated.

After registration, I began to unpack my things. It wasn't long until the first of my roommates walked through the door. This boy was tall, skinny, had red hair and a freckled complexion.

"I'm Derrick," he introduced. I returned the favor and shared my name.

"Where are you from, Derrick?" I asked.

"I'm from Dubai," he answered.

"Where's that?" I asked, with a look of curiosity.

"It's a country in the Middle East," Derrick said.

I couldn't believe he would come that far for a wrestling camp. Turns out, he lived in Dubai but came to the United States to help his grandparents in the summer, who happen to live in Michigan. A few moments later, my third roommate, a guy about my height with a stocky build, came through the door. He sported black hair and a pencil-thin mustache and wore a black t-shirt and jeans. He introduced himself as Nathaniel.

Unfortunately, we only had time for a short introduction before we had to head off to our first session. As per tradition, my lean, mean, green, machine was waiting for me outside the door. I received some curious looks and raised eyebrows from my roommates. I walked into the room and spotted some old, familiar faces and some new ones, too. Zach, CJ, and Coach Borelli all made an appearance.

During the warm-ups, I was having a particularly hard time with the exercises due to the amount of pain I was in. Despite all that, I pressed on. I looked around and noticed I was the only one left that was still trying to complete the last exercise. All of a sudden, the entire team of campers erupted in cheers and applause, encouraging me to keep going.

I managed to get through the first session, even with severe pain in my Achilles tendon. Because of the muscle contracture in my left foot, I cannot bring my heel to the floor. This can sometimes cause pain because I can't relax my foot. I got back to my room and collapsed onto the bed.

"Do you mind if I ask why you walk like that?" Derrick asked.

"I have cerebral palsy," I said. I told him my story about my birth and how I got into wrestling. Derrick's response was pretty much the same I got from everyone.

"That is amazing!" he exclaimed.

The week seemed to fly by in the blink of an eye and, before anyone knew it, it was time for the end of camp tournament. Unfortunately, my weight class was small, so I was only going to be able to have one match. With CJ as the referee, I stepped on the line to begin my bout with an extremely tall individual. I viciously grabbed onto his leg, but it wasn't long before he balled me up into a cradle.

I managed to fight out, but was never able to gain control of the match. I ended up losing after he attempted the cradle a second time. After the match, I walked over to the cooler to get a drink. I finished and was about to head back when I felt a hand on my shoulder. Standing behind me was a kid about my age with that all-to-familiar curious look on his face. I don't mind people asking questions, but you learn to recognize when people want to versus when they don't want to.

"My name is Tyler," he said. "Do you mind if I ask what's wrong with your legs?"

"I have cerebral palsy," I said.

"Oh! I thought you were retarded," he blurted out.

Retarded – that word makes my skin crawl. A word that insults those who, most of the time, can't defend themselves, and yet those individuals see the world in a clearer picture than anyone else ever could.

"No, I'm not," I responded. "I just have a physical disability."

He then began to ask me many more questions about my disability, so I shared my story with him. By the end of our conversation, he was asking for my phone number and a picture.

"By the way," I said. "You may want to choose a different word to use the next time you talk to someone with a disability."

I gathered my things and started to walk towards the dorm when a voice stopped me in my tracks. It was Chase, who had been one of my counselors every year I was at camp.

"Hey, Trevor," he said. "Will I see you next year?"

The reality of it all suddenly hit me. This was the very last time I would be able to attend camp.

"I'm a senior this year," I said as I embraced Chase in a hug.

"Whatever you do in life, I'm sure you'll be excellent," he said.

I rounded up my things and headed back to Ohio. I began to reflect on all of the good times I had over the years at the camp and how everyone was so good to me. If this is how I felt now, I couldn't imagine what it was going to be like when I had to hang it up for good.

23

Crossroads of Destiny

September 2015 – February 2016

"I've learned that a positive attitude isn't a technique for making your life perfect overnight. It's a lifestyle that takes time to develop and produce the positive changes you seek."

- Stan Toler

"I have wiped out your transgressions like a thick cloud and your sins like a heavy mist. Return to Me, for I have redeemed you."

Isaiah 44:22 (NASB)

Through all the excitement that wrestling brings, my church attendance became very hit and miss. I was continuing to go every now and again, but my friends stopped going, so why should I keep going? Out of the blue, they started going again, and I wanted to join them. For whatever reason, they decided to stop going to the church we were going to. It was rough, because I liked the church I was going to and didn't want to change. As we were riding down the road, I spotted a sign that said, "Crossroads Church." We rounded the bend and uncovered the trees to reveal a huge brick building.

As I approached the entrance, I was greeted by smiles and handshakes. The size of the church was quite intimidating. The lobby was as big as most country church sanctuaries. I walked into the sanctuary, and chairs were spread from one end of the sanctuary to the other. We sat down and waited for the pastor to get up on stage. Ironically, this pastor's name was Tim, too. I sat, rather bored, through the sermon. I couldn't wait to get home, but something about this church made me want come back again.

That's just what I did. Even when my friends stopped going, I continued. Everyone at Crossroads was so friendly and loving that I couldn't stay away. One morning, Pastor Tim announced there was going to be a revival service at the church and Stan Toler was going to be preaching. I had heard about revival services but had never actually been to one.

It was the second night of revival before I was finally able to go. I showed up half an hour early but didn't expect much. I thought revivals were just extra Sunday morning services. The service started and, after the worship music stopped, Stan got up to preach. I blocked out most of Stan's sermon, but there was one moment where his words pierced my soul. In that very moment, I realized I was not where I needed to be with God. I recalled getting saved a couple years prior, but my attitude hadn't changed. I was still cursing and feeding my mind things that would eventually destroy me.

I felt God tugging at my heart; it was as if I was literally being pulled to the altar. I fell to my knees, and Pastor Tim quickly joined my side to pray with me. With his guidance, I rededicated my life and fully surrendered to the Lord, and God instantly gave me a renewed focus. As I opened my eyes and stood up, Stan made his way over to me.

"What has the Lord done for you, son?" he asked.

"I am assured that I am saved," I said.

He looked at me with that classic grin and said, "Praise the Lord!"

***

A couple years later, in April of 2017, I had the privilege of seeing Dr. Toler on his "Revive America" tour with the gospel music group, The Guardians. Since the 2015 revival, Stan had been diagnosed with cancer. After the concert, he began greeting a crowd of people in the church lobby. I wasn't going to approach him due to the number of people in line, but the Lord pressed it on my heart to go up to him, shake his hand, and say thank you. I almost didn't, thinking I would have another chance but felt the tug to go up and talk to him.

"I just want to thank you. Because of you, I rededicated my life to the Lord," I said.

"I remember you. Praise the Lord!" he replied.

I'm glad I listened to the Holy Spirit that night, because just a few months later, Stan would lose his battle to cancer. Stan dedicated his life in service to the Lord Jesus Christ, and he would want you to know that today is the day of salvation. He led thousands to Christ and inspired millions all over the world. Make no mistake, Stan is not in Heaven because of works alone. No, he is in Heaven because of the blood Christ shed on Calvary to save mankind from their sins.

Stan Toler – Short in stature. A giant in the faith.

Something in the Water – February 2016

In the months that followed my rededication to Christ, I began to meet weekly with my youth pastor. After I went through the discipleship program, God laid it on my heart to get baptized. I let Pastor Tim know I wanted to be baptized and was glad to hear he'd be happy to do it. During the weeks before my baptism, I prayed and did my best to soften up my parents to come to church with me to watch me get baptized. My mother came, but my father did not.

On the day of my baptism, I guess I was a little bit nervous. As I was getting ready to enter the baptismal, I had forgotten that I didn't take my shoes off. Some gasps from the crowd indicated that something wasn't right, and I slipped my shoes off just before my big toe hit the water. Once I was in the pool, I waded my way over to Pastor Tim. This was it – I was about to make a public declaration to the world that I was a committed follower of Jesus Christ. There was no turning back; neither was there a desire to turn back on my part. I was ready for whatever God had in store for me.

"Trevor, do you profess Jesus Christ as your personal Lord and Savior?" Pastor Tim asked.

"I do," I responded.

"Then I baptize you in the name of the Father, of the Son and of the Holy Spirit."

Pastor Tim dunked me under the water, and I arose from the water to a sea of cheers and applause. I felt a sense of joy that will never be matched. The old man was drowning beneath my feet, while the new man was resuscitated for a new purpose. I had decided to follow Jesus, and there was no way I was going to turn back.

Beyond the Mat

Maybe you're like me: Maybe you are just going through the motions in your walk with Christ. You went to the altar and got saved, but afterward, there was no real change in your life. You go to church on Sunday and Wednesday, but you go right back to your sinful lifestyle the other days of the week. Friend, that is a dangerous way to live. You can't serve two masters.

You might be thinking, "I can still sin, and God will forgive me." God will indeed forgive us when we sin, but God's grace is not a free pass to sin and do whatever you want. God's grace gives us victory over sin we know is wrong and the things we had no idea we were doing wrong.

I had been taking advantage of God's grace by using it as a free pass to sin. I was using it as a crutch to continue doing the things I knew were wrong, but I did it anyway. I got saved, but I didn't make any attempt to grow in my relationship with God. Is that you? Are you just going through the motions? You can have victory over the sins you intentionally commit. All you have to do is fully surrender to God, and He will help you have victory.

Your relationship with God is the most important thing in your life. It is even above sports or anything else you put above God! Once you start to grow in your relationship with God, doors will start to open like you wouldn't imagine!

The day of my baptism with pastor Tim Throckmorton

24

Angels Among Us

October 2015

The angel of the Lord encamps around those who fear Him and rescues them.

Psalm 34:7 (NASB)

The last bell of the school day rang, and I raced to my car to get home. Traveling down State Route 56 with Air1 blaring on the radio, I couldn't help but think of how awesome my senior year was going to be. Not only that, but I had started working with another boy with cerebral palsy on his physical fitness. I turned on the final stretch of road to get to my house and gunned the gas pedal. I rounded a sharp curve but didn't even think about slowing down. Before I knew it, my car hit the bank, went airborne and flipped through the air.

My head bounced off the ceiling as my car landed on its top, and my driver side and back window exploded under the pressure before landing back on its wheels.

I sat still as the radio played, trying to process what just happened. I had a cut on my arm from the driver side window and I felt a stabbing pain where I hit my head. A quick inspection indicated that I had a laceration that would probably require stitches. I inspected all of my joints; nothing appeared to be broken. Then, I came to realization that my parents were going to kill me! I think I'd rather have broken a bone.

I made all the necessary calls, and the EMS arrived a short time later. I told the EMT about my head, and she began to inspect it.

"I don't see anything wrong." she said.

I was dumbfounded, because I knew I had an injury, I saw it myself and I showed her the blood on my hand.

"There's nothing there," she affirmed.

I was being loaded in the back of the squad when my parents came. To my relief, they didn't kill me. They were just glad I was okay. As I was walking out of the squad, an EMT stopped me and said, "You're pretty lucky, kid."

There are some things in life where the only explanation is divine intervention. Luck had nothing to do with it. There have been several situations in my life that should've turned out worse than they did. No weapon formed against me will prosper, this I know to be true. Why God chose to have such an imprint on my life is still a mystery to me. Truly, angels are among us.

25

An Unstoppable Will

December 2015 – January 2016

Therefore we also, since we are surrounded by so great a cloud of witnesses, let us lay aside every weight, and the sin which so easily ensnares us, and let us run with endurance the race that is set before us.

Hebrews 12:1 (NJKV)

Kenny Chesney did it right when he penned the song, "Don't Blink." Before I knew it, I was walking into the wrestling barn for my last first day of practice. I only had one win under my belt and, it being my senior year, I wanted more than anything to change that. I wanted to go out with a bang. The only difference is, this year, I didn't have Thomas along for the ride. However, I still had Micah, and he had the same mindset I did. We both wanted to leave our mark on not only our team, but the entire school.

Circleville Kiwanis – 12/5/15

The first stop on my quest to cement my legacy was a familiar one. We were going up against long-time rival, Circleville. Unfortunately, my first attempt at my quest didn't turn out like I'd hoped. As a matter of fact, I barely made it to the end of the first period in any of my matches. To make matters worse, at the end of the night, I once again was beaten by Greg Brewer. Greg and I had wrestled each other throughout most of my career, and every time we've stepped onto the mat thus far, he's beaten me. It was a pretty one-sided rivalry, but I always looked forward to wrestling him. Thus, ended my first attempt in to win a match, but it was only the beginning.

West Jefferson – 12/28/15

It is an unwritten rule in wrestling, "Thou shalt never start a wrestling meet on time." It never fails, no matter where we go, no matter how organized the tournament is, you can bet that there will be a delay of some kind. West Jefferson was no exception. It was an hour's drive up there, and the meet itself was delayed an hour and a half. This tournament invited some of the toughest competition of the year. It was going to be tough to get a win but not impossible. However, it didn't pan out like I hoped. I was able to last into the second period in a couple of my matches, but I still got pinned in all of them. It was hard to hide my disappointment, and yet, I gave myself no other choice but to keep moving forward.

Circleville Dual – 1/7/16

The next meet on the calendar was the dual meet against Circleville. This meant that I was only going to have one match for the night, and it was going to be against none other than Greg Brewer. I knew my chances of beating him were slim, but I was still going to give it my best shot. We took our places on the mat, shook hands, and the referee blew the whistle. I dropped to my knees and attacked his leg. I was only able to hold him for a few seconds before he broke free and got the takedown. I fought as hard as I could, but I was not able to escape the 45-second pin. And so, our final match with one another ended in quite the anticlimactic fashion.

Logan Elm Invitational, Day 1 – 1/8/16

After the disappointing loss from the day before, it was time to shift my focus to my favorite tournament of the season.

How poetic it would be if I was able to get a win on my home turf.

My first match of the weekend was up against a kid from Zane Trace. He wore one of those funny facemasks to protect his face, which meant the cross face wasn't going to work this time around. We locked up, and he quickly spun behind me to get the two. From there, he locked in the chicken wing and turned me onto my back with ease. I fought with all of my might but was still pinned in 55 seconds. This wasn't exactly how I wanted to start my last Logan Elm tournament.

My second match followed shortly after. Once the whistle blew, I dropped to my knees, but was again out-quickened when my opponent spun around me to get the takedown. He locked in the half nelson and turned me on my back. I heard the referee begin his count and began to fight ferociously. In the end, I was again pinned in the first period in 1:13.

At this point, my goal now was to at least make it out of the first period. I walked out to the mat for my third match of the day, more determined than ever to give this guy the fight of his life. The match started, and I immediately grabbed his leg. He tried to spin around me, but I used his momentum against him and wrapped my other arm around his body. I nearly got the takedown, but he broke free from my grip and got the takedown himself. I grabbed his leg once again until the referee called a stalemate.

At the restart of the match, we got into the referee's position. The ref blew the whistle, and my opponent instantly drove me to my stomach. I began to dig my elbows into the mat, trying to crawl out of bounds to escape. The ref blew the whistle to stop the match, and we returned to the referee's position. My opponent once again drove me flat to the ground and tried to sink in the half. Sensing the danger, I peeled his hand off of my neck. I cranked on his arm and almost had him flipped over before the referee signaled the end of first period.

Seeing that it was my choice to pick the position, I chose top. I mounted, and once the referee blew the whistle, I reared back and hit him with the hardest cross face I could muster. He immediately crumpled to the mat. I had the perfect opportunity to go for a pin! I desperately tried to lock in the half and turn him over, but he was able to stand up on one leg.

I took the opportunity to grab his other leg and drive him to the mat. In the middle of driving him, however, my back gave out, and my opponent was able to flip me completely over from the upright position. I thrashed and fought with everything I had, but I got pinned in the middle of the second period. I knew I came really close to winning that time.

Logan Elm Invitational, Day 2 – 1/9/16

The next morning it was safe to say my body was mad at me. I was sore from head to toe. I couldn't think about the soreness, I had another day of wrestling ahead of me. In a way, I felt rejuvenated. Especially after my last match from the day before.

My first match of the day was a kid from Amanda. He quickly got me down on the ground and attempted to pin me. I was able to fight out of the pin and roll onto my belly. From there, I grabbed onto his leg and tried to pull myself back onto my knees, but he quickly spun, switched to my right side, and tried to lock in the half. I was able to fight out of it, get to my hands and knees, and flip him over top of me, nearly putting him on his back. However, I wasn't quick enough to turn into him and get the takedown. This led to him regaining control and putting me back to square one. I was once again on my back, fighting for my life. Thankfully, the period ended a few seconds later, keeping me in the match.

I was so tired already; I could barely stand up. I chose to go top, but my opponent turned into me and broke me down before I could hit the cross face. He quickly rolled me onto my back, but I was able to keep my shoulders off the mat for the minute and a half left in the period. I made it to the third period, but I had to drag myself over to the center circle. My opponent easily flattened me to the mat and rolled me onto my back. I was able to fight for about thirty seconds before being pinned in the middle of the third period.

I was completely exhausted, but I still had two more matches to go. My second match came, and he was quick and wiry. I fought as hard as I could, but he was able to get the best of me in 1:30. In my third and final match of the weekend, I only managed to get taken down once and managed to fight getting pinned until the end of the third period. After my matches, I walked back to the locker room.

Alone, I sat down, smiled, and reflected about how much fun it was getting the daylights beat out of me and realized how much I was going to miss it when it was over.

26

A Brave Send-off

February 2016

Rejoice in the Lord always; again, I will say, rejoice! Let your gentle spirit be known to all men. The Lord is near.

Philippians 4:4-5 (NASB)

The season was passing by quicker than I ever could've imagined. It seemed like only yesterday we were starting the first meet of the season, and here we were, two weeks away from sectionals. The trouble now was making it to sectionals. A freshman on my team moved up to the 138-pound weight class, which just so happens to be the class I'm in. He ended up beating me in the wrestle-off, which pretty much ruined my chances of wrestling at the upcoming tri-meet. To make matters worse, it was going to be the last home meet of the season.

I thought my hopes were dashed, but Coach Daniels came up to me after practice with an offer I couldn't refuse.

"We have a hole in the 152-pound slot, and we need a full team for the meet," he said. "Do you want to fill it?"

"Absolutely!" I said.

"You have to weigh in at 141 on Thursday," Coach Daniels said.

It was currently Monday, and I weighed 136. I smiled as I thought to myself, *I now have the problem every wrestler dreams of having. I actually have to eat if I want to be able to wrestle.* This was still going to be a challenge for me. Because my body expends so much energy, it is easier for me to lose weight than to gain. Over the next few days, I gorged myself and probably drank enough water to fill a swimming pool all in a desperate attempt to make weight.

The moment of truth finally arrived. I continued to drink water as an added precaution until right before I needed to weigh in. I stepped on the scale and held my breath as it calculated. After a few seconds, the scale read 141.2 lbs. I made it over the first hurdle, but the battle was far from over. I walked out of the locker room, and a surreal feeling came over me. This was going to be last time I would ever step on the mat at Logan Elm.

People began to file in as the matches started. It seemed like forever to hear my weight class called, but it did finally arrive. My opponent and I shook hands, and we locked up. For some unknown reason, the referee blew the whistle to stop the match, and we had to start over. We locked up again, and he easily spun around me for the takedown. Afterwards, he let me back up to get the escape and took me back down again. I could definitely sense a speed difference and feel the twelve-pound weight difference, but that wasn't an excuse not to try my hardest. He locked me in a chicken wing and rolled me onto my back. I fought my hardest, but he was still able to pin me in the first period.

During the break before my final match, Mom came up to me and pointed me in the direction of the crowd. The student section was packed full of kids holding up signs. One of which read, "Trevor Lane: Congratulations on an amazing wrestling career!" I was so deeply touched but at the same time, it made me realize that my next match was my final one at home.

My second match was against Amanda Clearcreek. How appropriate it was that my debut match in 2010 was against them, and I was now wrestling my final home match in 2016 against Amanda Clearcreek. It came all too quickly. My teammates sent me out, my opponent and I shook hands, and the match began. Much like last time, my opponent quickly took me down only to let me back up and take me down again. He rolled me onto my back with ease and pinned me in the first period.

I couldn't help but be a little disappointed. It seemed like an anticlimactic end for a last home match. However, I did not expect what would happen next. Everyone in the gym rose to their feet in cheers and applause. My opponent, after shaking my hand, embraced me in a hug. Austin, a person on the Amanda Clearcreek team I had wrestled against my entire career, came out and hugged me as well. The rest of the Amanda team soon followed as well as my own band of brothers, who all embraced me.

The meet concluded with Logan Elm's defeat, but after everything settled down, my teammates and I all gathered in a circle. I hugged each person, and then Nick spoke up. He reached into his bag and pulled out a replica WWE Intercontinental championship belt. On it were the signatures of all my teammates and coaches.

"We appreciate all that you've done," Nick said.

I was so shocked, all I could muster was, "Thank you."

At that moment, I realized I had something more special than winning any one match. I was telling my story and inspiring everyone around me. Every time I stepped onto the mat, I won. I was undefeated against cerebral palsy. In my 18 years of life, I had already encountered many detours and traffic jams on the road of life. I was quickly approaching a four-way stop and would have to choose where to turn next. Wrestling was quickly coming to an end. Many could choose to look at my wrestling career and call it a failure in terms of accolades, but it's the journey, not necessarily the destination, that makes you who you are.[1] Two more weeks.

---

[1] Hartman, A. (2015, February 26). Wrestler Shares Inspiring Journey Of Overcoming Cerebral Palsy To Embody The True Meaning Of Resilience.

27

Full Circle

February 2016

Two are better than one, because they have a good reward for their labor. For if they fall, one will lift up his companion. But woe to him who is alone when he falls, for he has no one to help him up. Again, if two lie down together, they will keep warm; But how can one be warm alone? Though one may be overpowered by another, two can withstand him. And a threefold cord is not quickly broken.

Ecclesiastes 4:9-12 (NKJV)

The next stop was St. Charles Prep School in Bexley, Ohio. This was the final meet before sectionals and, while I wasn't worried as much about winning a match, it was still in the back of my mind. Thankfully, I was able to drop back down to 138 for this meet, so I was on a more even playing field. The school itself was small and very old. When we got there, we were crammed like sardines into a small gym with dozens of other wrestlers and only two wrestling mats. Adjacent to this gym was another slightly larger gym which housed three more wrestling mats. It was going to be an interesting day, to say the least.

The meet started, and my first match came up rather quickly. My first opponent of the day was from Westfall. I dropped to my knees, and he reached out and palmed my head. I swatted his hand away and dove for the leg. Now I was in the predicament that I almost always found myself in – I couldn't get up on my knees to get the takedown. Because of this, he was able to spin around me and score a takedown. He started to turn me over, and I resisted as long as I could, but in the end, I got pinned in the first period. I got to my feet and shook hands with my opponent. As I was walking off the mat, the referee patted me on the shoulder in a job well done.

That certainly wasn't the way I wanted the meet to start out, but I knew I had another chance. Part of the process of losing is understanding another opportunity will present itself through persistence, not pity. My second match of the day came, and I was determined to make the most of this opportunity. Once the match started, I was instantly locked into a front headlock and scored on. I grabbed onto the leg and held on for dear life. I was almost able to get behind him and get a takedown myself, but my opponent got to his feet and behind me again before that could happen. Surprisingly, I was able to muster enough strength to stand up, get out of his grip and get an escape point. We locked up again only for my opponent to score another takedown and take me to my back for back points. This sequence of moves finished out the first period.

At the beginning of the second period, I chose to go top. As soon as the whistle blew, I pounded him with a cross face, but he was able to turn and face me. In order to prevent him from getting an escape point, I grabbed onto his leg. The attempt was a failure, however, because like a slithering snake, he was able to wiggle free from my grip.

Although he got the escape, I kept ahold of his head, grabbed the inside of his leg, and drove him down to the mat as hard as I could. The result: a takedown! He tried to stand up, but I would not let go. However, just like that, my opponent used my own momentum to propel me onto my back to get the pin fall. I was not at all disappointed with that match, but like always, it was time to move on.

By the time my third and final match of the day came around, I was beginning to feel the fatigue. I locked up with my opponent, and he easily spun around me for a takedown. After a few seconds, he very carefully and slowly let me back up for an escape. Something was very strange. His movements were very soft and slow. It suddenly dawned on me that he was taking it easy on me! I became enraged. You can stare at me, you can make fun of me, but I will not stand for pity! At the start of the second period, my opponent appeared to not even try to get an escape. Instead, he stood on one knee and looked to his coach for instruction while I held onto his leg getting back to my base. He tried desperately to break my grip but couldn't.

Before we knew it, it was time for the third period. My opponent chose the neutral position, and we locked up yet again. He was able to get the takedown pretty quickly but spent the rest of the round trying to roll me over into a pin. After nearly two minutes of fighting, he was finally able to get the pin.

At the conclusion of the match, I walked back in the hallway towards the other gym. I was still fuming over the fact that the person I just wrestled quite possibly gave me less than his best, and he still beat me. Suddenly, I felt a hand on the back of my shoulder. I turned around, and it was the person I had just wrestled, and he was breathless.

"You're so strong," he said in between breaths. "I couldn't get you over. People like you inspire me so much. Thank you!"

I was shocked at what happened next, as he embraced me in a hug. All of my anger quickly melted away, and I returned the hug. Maybe he gave it his best, after all.

"Thank you," I said. "That means a lot."

I walked over to my mom in the auxiliary gym, and she was very unusually focused on a match.

"Look over there," she said, pointing over to the far-left mat. "Does that boy have cerebral palsy?"

After a closer look, I observed one of the boys wrestling was stumbling quite a bit, and he was walking on his toes with his right foot.

"Yes!" I exclaimed.

I walked over to his mat to get a closer look and discovered that it was tied, and there were only ten seconds left in the match. The boy quickly lunged forward, grabbed his opponents' leg, and scored the takedown before time was up, giving him the win. I was happy for him, but it felt strange. I just watched someone who knows exactly what I'm going through win a match, and, from his reaction, it wasn't his first. I was relieved, though, that there was someone else like me who was wrestling. I had to get to know him. I barely gave him a chance to catch his breath before I went over and talked to him.

"Hey, man, great job. I wrestle and have CP, too," I said.

"Really?" he asked, surprised. "Wrestling is the best thing you've ever done for yourself, isn't it," he said as if he could read my mind.

"Oh, yeah! For sure!" I said

He had to leave, but I was able to catch back up with him after the awards assembly. His name was Michael, and, as I suspected, his CP affected his right side. We spent a good ten minutes talking about the struggles we had growing up and how we got into wrestling. Often times, we need to be reminded that we are not alone in this fight, and this was my reminder. It was one of the most humbling experiences, watching someone going through the same thing you are win a wrestling match himself. As my final match grew ever closer, after watching and talking with Michael, I felt as if my career was coming full circle.

Beyond the Mat

No matter who you are, no matter where you come from, everyone, everywhere, needs to be reminded they are not alone. When you have a disability or are a caretaker of someone with a disability, it is very easy to feel isolated and alone. When I was a kid, I didn't know anybody older than me with cerebral palsy that I could look up to. I had an amazing support system, but nobody truly understood what I was going through because they didn't have CP themselves. I'm here to tell you today that if you're a young kid or an adult with cerebral palsy or some other disability, you are not alone!

28

LEaving A LEgacy

February 19th – 20th, 2016

Do you not know that in a race all the runners run, but only one gets the prize? Run in such a way as to get the prize. Everyone who competes in the games goes into strict training. They do it to get a crown that will not last, but we do it to get a crown that will last forever.

1 Corinthians 9:24-25 (NIV)

As I walked down the hall to my first period class, I stopped at my locker. Right as I was about to open the door, I found a note that simply read: "Good luck, Trevor!" The sectional tournament was already weighing heavy on my mind and this only intensified the matter. The day seemed to pass by at a snail's pace. I skipped study hall just so I could go down to the wrestling barn early, before anyone else got there. I sat on the bench and soaked in the silence. I reflected over the last six years and how far I had come. My teammates and coaches poured everything they had into me, and now it was time to focus on the legacy I wanted to leave behind.

About an hour later, the rest of my teammates began to file in. It was a 40-minute bus ride from Logan Elm to Washington Courthouse, where the first leg on the road to the state championship began. I so wanted time to slow down. I didn't want it to ever end. Once we arrived at the school, I retreated to the locker room. I took my time getting dressed, knowing that today could be the last day I ever put on a wrestling singlet as an active competitor. Of course, my goal was still to win.

The first round of the night kicked off, and my first match shortly followed. I walked out onto the mat with a renewed focus. I fully understood what was on the line. Not only was I fighting to keep my career in-tact, but I was also fighting for a chance to wrestle at districts and state. My career wasn't over until that final whistle blew.

The match started, and I dropped to my knees and attacked my opponents' leg. I struggled to pull myself up to get the takedown, and my opponent spun around me and got two. He locked the half nelson in and rolled me over. I fought with everything I had, but my opponent got the pin in 1:23 in the first period. My sense of desperation was growing as I realized that I only had one more chance to win, and if I lost, I was done for good. Fortunately, I had a bye the next round, which meant that I had wait until the next day to wrestle my next match.

Sectionals, Day 2 – 2/20/16

I woke up the next morning, grateful. Grateful that I had another day to spend with my brothers on the mat and grateful that I would don that singlet once again to wrestle. As I prepared for my match, mixed emotions flooded my mind.

"Are you ready, Trev?" Nick asked.

"As I'll ever be," I replied.

My name was called, and I ran to check in. I slowly walked out onto the mat, soaking in every moment, every sight, and every sound. Nick watched in the far corner as my opponent, and I stepped on the line. The whistle blew, and I tried to methodically plot my next move. Before I could react, though, my opponent had already gotten behind me and scored a takedown. I quickly crawled out of the circle to force the ref to stop the match. In the down position, I immediately stood up and got out for an escape point. I continued to pressure him, but he was able to get me flat on my stomach and hit me with a cross face before the period's end.

My opponent chose to take bottom in the second period. Once the whistle blew, I was able to follow him to his feet without losing my balance. My error came when I tried to pick him up for a slam and ended up falling on my side. This mess up enabled him to get the escape point. I was back to square one. I tried getting inside, but he was keeping his guard up and keeping his distance. What happened next was a series of three takedowns and escapes, followed by a pin attempt by my opponent. I fought and kicked with everything I had. If this was going to be my last match, my opponent was not going to get off that easy. I managed to fight out of the first pin attempt, but my opponent immediately transitioned to another one. I was not able to fight out, and the referee's hand hit the mat for the pin fall.

I slowly rose to my feet, and the crowd did the same in applause. After I shook my opponents' hand and took off my ankle bracelet, I stood in the middle of the circle for a short time, trying to process what just happened. I walked over to Coach Daniels and gave him a firm handshake.

"It's been a pleasure, Trevor," Coach Daniels said.

I then walked over to Nick and embraced him in a hug.

"Thank you for everything, Trev," he said. "I'll miss you."

As I walked around the perimeter of the mat, standing on the far-left side was my mom. I gave her a great big bear hug and held her for what seemed like a few minutes. Tears began to flow as reality came crashing down on me. I was never going to be able to put on a singlet and wrestle for Logan Elm ever again. I was never going to have another opportunity to have my hand raised in an official match, and I was never going to be able to make more memories, except for the ones I've already made.

I finally let go of my mom and greeted the others who were waiting.

"You've had one heck of a career, kid," Coach Polly said.

Other teammates, wrestlers, and spectators came to congratulate me on a job well done. As I was making my way through the sea of people, I noticed something strange. Random strangers were crying right along with me. It was in that moment I realized my legacy wasn't about wins, losses, or broken records. My legacy was about adapting and overcoming any challenge that came my way. All while inspiring countless numbers of people in the process. I didn't need to win a match to get approval or be successful; I just needed to share my story of overcoming cerebral palsy with God's help, despite what my doctors told me. That, my friends, makes me victorious.

Epilogue

March 2016 – January 2018

My frame was not hidden from You, When I was made in secret, And skillfully wrought in the lowest parts of the earth. Your eyes saw my substance, being yet unformed. And in Your book they all were written, The days ordained for me, When as yet there were none of them.

Psalm 139:15 – 16 (NKJV)

Chasing the Dream – March 2016

The amateur wrestling portion of my life came to a close, but that just meant that bigger and better things were on the horizon. Although, I wouldn't rule out the possibility of one more match if God allows. I would want it to be against another person with cerebral palsy. After that, I would be content on ending my wrestling career. Another way I would return to wrestling is if I had the opportunity to help someone else who has CP with their wrestling technique. Whether one of those doors opens or not, remains to be seen.

I wasted little time phasing into the next chapter of my life, though, in the pursuit of professional wrestling. I searched far and wide for the perfect wrestling school, but during my search, I thought to myself, *who on earth is going to have the patience to train someone with cerebral palsy?*

I continued searching until I found an advertisement for a pro-wrestling training session with Gregory Iron in Cleveland, Ohio. It just so happened Greg had cerebral palsy himself in his right side, so I thought he would be the perfect person to train me. I sent him a message, and the rest was history. He said he would be glad to train me. With the training session just a few days away, I begged my parents to let me go. Reluctantly, my parents agreed. As a bonus, my mentor, Ken, also lived in Cleveland, and I was going to get to meet him for the very first time.

After a three-hour journey, we finally arrived at the gym. As soon as I walked through the door, I was met with a ring right in the middle of the gym. I walked over and Greg was sitting on the ring apron. We introduced ourselves and Greg began to tell his story. He talked about how he suffered a stroke as a baby, which caused his cerebral palsy. He went on to say that he grew up in a broken home and never had much support. Especially when it came to pursuing his dream to be a professional wrestler.

If someone can go through all of that and still accomplish their dreams, then nothing should stop me from achieving mine.

My first challenge was trying to get into the ring. While most people step through the second rope to get in, I had to improvise and roll underneath the bottom rope. Once I was in the ring, I felt like a totally different person. The atmosphere was beyond exciting, and I felt as light as a feather. I was able to get through some of the warm-ups but struggled with others. Then came my first real test. Greg demonstrated a "bump," which is just falling backward to make it look like the guy hit you.

That seems simple enough. After all, I fall by accident all the time.

I took the proper form just as he had shown me and tumbled backward. Upon impact, my head collided with the ring with a thud. My skull was rattled, and it took me a few minutes to get my bearings. Being stubborn, I tried again and again and again. Each time, I failed. Greg must have sensed things weren't going well for me because we transitioned to the collar and elbow tie up. He demonstrated it, and I copied his demonstration.

"You're locking up better than most people who have been wrestling for a while," Greg said. "Tone it down on the intensity, though."

That was one of the most challenging things for me. In professional wrestling, the objective is to tell a story. You aren't supposed to be trying to kill your opponent, which is the exact opposite of amateur wrestling. After a few times, I was able to get the right tempo, and we moved onto the next exercise – running the ropes. This proved to be especially difficult. To run the ropes, you had to have your foot placement and timing on hitting the ropes just right. I tried dozens of times to try to get the timing right, but I never could. Still, I was eager to have one match with Greg.

"Go to college first," he said. "Realistically, chances are you won't make that great of a living on the independent scene, and you'll need something to fall back on."

I had every intention in the world of going to college. I wanted to become a physical therapist because I wanted to help kids in the same situation I was in. The session ended, and I still hadn't lost that fire to want to be a pro wrestler.

The next morning, I started to pack my bags to head home, but not before I met up with Ken. I was standing up against the wall in the lobby when he walked in. He was much shorter than I imagined, and he came hobbling in on a cane. We sat down and talked about everything from wrestling to ministry. Then he reached over and pulled out a gift bag and gave it to me. Inside were his wrestling boots. As our visit concluded, I promised him that if I ever had the opportunity to wrestle, I would use his boots in the match.

An Unforgettable Surprise – May 17th, 2016

Every year, Logan Elm hosts an awards ceremony for the seniors. They give out various scholarships and awards of recognition. One award that they give out is the Ohio High School Athletic Association (OHSAA) Courageous Student Award. This award is given to someone who has overcome great adversity in their life. My name was called to receive that award, and the reaction I got was nothing short of amazing. The entire student body rose to their feet in a standing ovation as I went forward to receive the certificate. I was touched to have such a reaction. To think that I could be an inspiration to so many people! You never know who is watching and how many lives you are touching.

Graduation – May 29th, 2016

The day every high school senior dreams of finally arrived – graduation day! It was bittersweet for me as I walked down the aisle to my chair. I couldn't help but think back to all of the amazing memories

I made throughout my tenure at Logan Elm. From kindergarten all the way up to senior year. The same people who were by my side in kindergarten, were the same people who were walking on stage with me.

I couldn't help but feel an overwhelming sense of gratitude to all of the people at Logan Elm – students and teachers included. I very rarely dealt with bullying, and I was never excluded from anything, even as a teenager. I truly had the best classmates in the world, and I am convinced that I wouldn't have turned out as well as I did if I went anywhere else. All of my physical therapists, occupational therapists, speech therapists, doctors, nurses, and surgeons were taken by surprise. My name was finally called, and I went up and received my diploma. The doctors told me I would never walk, never talk, never be able to do anything. Despite what they said, by the grace of God, I was able to adapt and overcome. I am alive and thriving, and now it was time to show the world what I could do.

Answering the Call to Ministry

That fall, I jumped straight into college at Hocking Community College and began to pursue a degree to become a Physical Therapist Assistant. It wasn't long, though, before I was met with my first hurdle. To get into the PTA program, you had to take one year of general courses and place in the top 30 of your class. I was never academically gifted, especially in math, but I was willing to do whatever it took to accomplish my goal. By the grace of God and with some amazing study buddies, I scraped by with a 3.0 and placed 27th in my class.

Once I was in the program, I did very well in the first half of the semester. However, then the practical side of the class came. We had to demonstrate the skills we learned. When demonstrating things like safe bed transfers and gait training, I would often lose my own footing. When it came to using some of the smaller tools, my hands would often shake, and I couldn't get an accurate measurement. Unfortunately, I ended up flunking out of PTA school. On the last day of school, I walked out of the classroom with my head hung low. However, God's timing is impeccable. As I boarded the elevator to leave, I heard God clearly say, "I want you to become an evangelist."

While all this was all going on, God also laid it on my heart to start a ministry for people with special needs at my church. I wrestled with this for weeks as I contemplated if this is what God wanted me to do. I asked God to give me a sign that He wanted me to start a disability ministry when I went to church on Sunday.

That Sunday morning, I walked into the narthex and was met by a man named Tim Tener. We exchanged greetings and further into our conversation he said, "You know, you ought to think about starting a ministry for people with disabilities. It is an extremely needed ministry and you seem like the perfect person for the job."

I couldn't believe what I just heard. Tim didn't even know that I was thinking about starting a disability ministry. Furthermore, he couldn't have known I asked God for a sign just a few days before our conversation because I was alone when I prayed that prayer. I took that as a sign from God and I took my idea to pastor Tim. He loved my idea and hooked me up with our newly hired youth pastor, Dan Coy to help develop the ministry.

Pastor Dan and I had many meetings around many restaurant tables. After many months of planning and strategizing God's Abled was born – with the mission being to help individuals with special needs reach their God-given potential. Dan and I were at McDonalds one day going over the final details before launch day.

"I want this outreach to go beyond this community," I told Dan.

Dan thought for a moment and said, "Have you ever heard of David Ring?"

"Yes, I have!" I said.

A few years prior, Ken had shown me a video of David, singing "What A Day That Will Be." He has cerebral palsy and can barely speak, but he was still on stage, singing. After watching, I wanted to meet him so badly, and the thought of doing ministry with him filled me with excitement.

God's Abled finally launched in June of 2017, and we only had one person show up. This person is on the Autism spectrum, and, as God would have it, she was also my student aide in pre-school. She had just recently given her heart to Christ but had no one to disciple her because she was kicked out of her church because of her behavior.

There is an old expression in the church world that God can make an ocean out of a river. I began to disciple her and help her find her best fit within the church. She is now one of the most faithful attendees, in the church and she serves and volunteers in many ways in the church. One of the most amazing ways I've seen God use her is through her need of providers. Because of her disability, she is not able to live totally on her own or drive. That is where a care provider comes in. A care provider will come in and check on her and take her places where she needs or wants to go – this includes church.

Interestingly enough, every provider she brought to church was anything but a Christian! Some of their backgrounds include atheist, Mormon, Muslim and even Wiccan! To fulfill their job as providers, they had to bring her to church and they got to hear the Gospel because she faithfully went to church every Wednesday and Sunday.

Leap of Faith

In the middle of trying to get a brand-new ministry off the ground, I was still wrestling with the fact that God was calling me preach the Gospel. After about a week of prayer, I decided to take my dilemma to Dan. As it stood, I couldn't learn how to preach at a secular community college. I told Dan that I felt God was calling me to preach and asked for his advice.

"I've sensed that about you," Dan affirmed. "Why don't you try God's Bible School and College? They have an amazing track record of training excellent ministers!"

I prayed for a long time about what God wanted me to do. I figured the least I could do while trying to figure out what to do was visit the campus. Dan had a lot of connections on campus and he graciously went with me on the tour. It was an hour and a half drive from Circleville to Cincinnati. The commute alone was a turn off to me because that meant I wouldn't have enough time to run my ministry back home. Still, I kept an open heart and mind.

We traveled several hilly and winding roads before we reached the college on top of a steep hill – "The Hilltop" as it was called. Once I stepped on campus, I could instantly tell the school possessed quite a bit of history and more importantly, I felt the presence of God. Admittedly, I struggled with a bit of culture shock. The on-campus dress code was very traditional where a suit and tie was regularly worn attire. I stuck out like a sore thumb in my blue jeans and t-shirt. Fortunately, the nervousness quickly faded when I discovered how nice everyone was.

The first of the faculty I had the privilege of meeting were Dr. Mark Bird and Dr. Alan Brown. Both were incredibly brilliant men who told some amazing stories of how God has worked in and through GBS. The school was founded in 1900 by Martin Wells Knapp and it was literally deeded to God! My interest to attend was certainly peaked when I learned of the history of the school and the deal was sealed when I found out I could attend online. I wouldn't have to leave Circleville or stop my ministry. This was a sure sign that God wanted me to attend GBS and I enthusiastically enrolled.

As I am writing this, I am currently in my junior year at God's Bible School, pursuing a bachelor's degree in biblical and theological studies. The Lord has used this time to strengthen my faith and prepare me for deeper ministry down the road. I cannot wait to see what He has in store.

Pushing Ahead

Despite many months of low numbers, we pressed on because God had a plan. Dan and I decided in order to supplement the financial needs of the ministry, we would need to host a fundraiser. This would be the perfect opportunity to bring in David Ring. In January of 2018, we launched the fundraising banquet with David Ring. Before we went up to speak, he pulled me off to the side.

"I am very interested in partnering with you," he said.

I couldn't believe the doors God was opening. After we finished the banquet, David came and preached the next morning. His testimony touched my heart, and he is a prime example of God's love and amazing grace. After the service, I helped him load his things into his car. We finished, and he turned to me.

"Don't you quit on me, or I'm going to kick your butt," he said.

As I watched him drive away, I thought back to all that I had been through and the doors God opened and was opening because of those circumstances. Then I recalled a story I heard my mom tell some years back. Shortly before I was born, my mom lay alone in her hospital room, scared of what the future would hold (keep in mind, it was too late to do an ultra-sound to see if I was a boy or a girl). In the stillness of the night, my mom felt someone place His hand on her shoulder and heard a voice that said, "Don't worry, he will be all right."

I don't know about you, but I'd say I turned out all right.

Final Thought

I hope you enjoyed reading my story. As you read my story, I hope you were inspired but more importantly, I hope you saw evidence of how amazing God is. It may have crossed your mind that it looks as if my life has been planned out – that's because it has. Jeremiah 1:5 says, "Before I formed you in the womb, I knew you…" (NKJV).

Before I was born, God saw that I was going to be born premature. He saw what I was going through as a child, all the struggles and pain. You may ask, if God is so good, why would He allow a sick child to live only to force him to live with a physical disability?

It is important to remember that we live in a fallen, broken world. No one is immune to suffering, not even Jesus. When Adam and Eve gave into the temptation to eat the forbidden fruit and disobeyed God, the world fell into sin. Because the world is in a state of brokenness, anyone that is born into a broken world, is broken themselves. However, God can take something the devil meant for evil and turn it around for good (Romans 8:28).

It's true God saw that I was going to have CP and the challenges associated with it. However, He also saw that I was going to have amazing parents and family that wouldn't take no for an answer. He saw all the friends I was going to make. True, genuine friends that liked me for who I was and not because they felt sorry for me.

I consider Cerebral palsy the greatest blessing of my life. All of the things I have experienced in my life have shaped me into who I am today. Without CP, the story you just read would not have been possible.

To those of you reading this, I don't know what you've been through in your life, but God wants to take your brokenness and pain and turn it into something beautiful. I am a sinner that has been redeemed by the blood of Jesus. There is nothing extraordinary about me, but I serve an extraordinary God that has completely turned my life around. It is nothing that I've done, but everything that He has done within me. God wants to do and can do an amazing work in your life, just as He has done in mine.

All you have to do is repent of your sins and ask Jesus into your heart. You say, "I'm a good person." You might be a good person by your standards, but how about God's? If you have broken any one of the 10 commandments in your life, you will not be able to go to Heaven. You will not be able to ask for forgiveness of your sins on judgement day. By then, it will be too late. That's why God sent His Son, Jesus to die on the cross for the sins of the world. He knew that we as imperfect humans were incapable of keeping all His commandments.

The Bible says, all who call upon the name of the Lord shall be saved (Acts 2:21, Romans 10:13). How do you call upon the name of the Lord to be saved? It's as easy as A-B-C!

A – Admit to God that you are a sinner and ask Jesus to forgive you of your sins.

B – Believe that Jesus is who He says He is – that He was born of a virgin, lived a perfect life, was crucified for the sins of the world and rose again three days later declaring victory over death.

C – Confess Him as the Lord and Savior of your life and begin to grow in the grace and knowledge of Jesus Christ.

If you prayed a prayer like that and are serious, find a Bible believing church in your area and begin to grow in grace and knowledge. You will be amazed at how God will use you. If you are still skeptical, I pray that reading my story has at least made you think. Christ's return is very soon, and I want as many people as possible to come to Heaven with me. I won't have Cerebral palsy anymore and I'm looking forward to running down the streets of gold with you!

Coach Hurd

Meeting Michael

David Ring and Trevor

President of Joni and Friends, John Nugent

About the Author

Trevor currently resides in Circleville, Ohio and is in his junior year at God's Bible School and College in Cincinnati, Ohio. Trevor began speaking publicly in schools and other venues as well as preaching the Gospel in 2016. More recently, he has began speaking all over the United States, sharing the Gospel and advocating for people affected by disability. He is also developing God's Abled into a global ministry to reach people affected by disability with the Gospel all over the world.

If you're interested in having Trevor speak at your church, school or other event, or if you have a comment or about his book he can be reached at: **godsabled13@gmail.com**

Made in the USA
Monee, IL
19 April 2022